Unmasking
Grief

*A Guide for Women Navigating
the Emotional Journey of
Grieving and Losing a Loved One*

Alison Brehme

For more information, hello@alisonbrehme.com

ISBN: 979-8-89109-260-0 - paperback
ISBN: 979-8-89109-261-7 - ebook

Get Your Free Gifts!

To get the best experience with this book, I've found readers who download these free *Unmasking Grief* resources feel more encouragement and support while grieving the loss of a loved one.

DOWNLOAD YOUR FREE GIFTS!

You can get a copy by visiting:
www.alisonbrehme.com/grief

Contents

Author's Note

Grief is a complex topic to write about. It's so personal. But we need to look farther under the hood and understand that any emotion we are experiencing is okay and that other people are probably experiencing the same thing too. And what a relief, because that will allow us to find freedom instead of judging our journeys (or each other).

Think about your favorite character in a movie. The main characters are always on a journey, right? For example: Frodo in *Lord of the Rings*, Luke Skywalker in *Star Wars,* and Princess Buttercup in *The Princess Bride.* They each went on a journey, and encountered many obstacles along the way. On top of that, they had to wage war against their outward enemies and their inner demons. The same thing is true of grief.

Grieving is a journey with a winding, lengthy path. There will be phases of peace, joy, heartache, and pain. Most movie characters go through an inward and an outward battle. That's what facing grief will look like as well.

This is even more true as women of faith, who have an added expectation to always seem put together. It creates a facade. We're all wearing masks, myself included.

When we have these human moments, sharing our past and painful experiences with one another is another way to connect with others. People are tired of being preached at—they want reality. To see that you made it out to the other side of your trauma with hope still in your hand can be just as powerful as someone preaching from a pulpit. Sharing our stuff, even when we aren't proud of our choices, could minister in a way where people see God differently. They see God's goodness, peace, and love because if you still believe in God after everything you've been through, then to someone else, that can be life-changing.

I believe in God. I believe in a Higher Power. I know there is something bigger than myself out there. So you'll see these ideals referenced throughout the book. I grew up in a Christian household. But that doesn't mean that I never questioned my faith! I spent years not going to church. I spent years making stupid and selfish choices. I thought that I was coping. I thought I was handling my business. But I wasn't. I was hiding. All that pretending piled up and caused havoc in multiple areas of my life.

I always felt that even though I've had crappy things happen in my life, there has been a spiritual force present. I felt there was a "being" who had my back, and that was God. And believe me, my relationship with God has not always been solid. It's been a rocky road with sprinkles of anger, confusion, and skepticism. But even though it's been difficult at times, I have been grateful for everything in my life and what I've gone through because it was ultimately for me.

Whatever or whoever you believe in, there is a world out there larger than ourselves. We are on this earth for a purpose, and sometimes, the painful things we go through can lead us to our designated path. And those who come across our way may be placed there intentionally so that we can support them as they go through this life journey.

That means you have an important part to play. No one can grieve for you.

Grief is an intense topic, and you may not feel like reading this book cover to cover in one sitting. You may not feel like reading it to the end at all. Both of those things are okay. Take your time with it. Think through the questions posed within these pages. Sometimes, answers will take time to come to you. They may take a day or week to find you. But, by the end of this book, the hope is that you will:

- Discover that there is more to grief than meets the eye.
- Understand that your thoughts and feelings are okay, even when you're angry and questioning your faith.
- Adopt a new technique or have a mindset shift that helps you when you feel emotionally overwhelmed.
- Get extra support through a coach, counselor, or licensed professional, knowing it is brave and sometimes needed to help us process what's happening.

Introduction

L ife can be overwhelming. If you are alive and breathing, then you've experienced grief in some form or fashion. Typically grief is most commonly thought of as an emotion that comes about when someone passes away. But it's more complex and can show up under any circumstance:

- Death of a spouse, child, parent, friend, or loved one
- Separation or divorce
- Suicide
- Diagnosis of a disease, chronic illness, or health issue
- Loss of business, job, or promotion, or career change
- Financial loss
- Loss of home or property (foreclosure, natural disaster)
- Loss of a pet
- Loss of friendship
- Romantic breakup
- Abortion/miscarriage
- Significant life changes (graduation, retirement)
- Imprisonment
- Global events (politics, pandemics)
- Racial and social injustice

Have you gone through any of these? Sometimes, grief is a sudden loss. It's out of the blue and stops you completely in your tracks. But, on the other hand, it could also be caused by something that's anticipated or expected. Either way, these losses cause shock and trauma.

Here's the thing: we weren't taught how to grieve. So instead, you emulate what you've seen others do in your life, which just leaves you with more questions than answers. Next, you turn to Google and look for information on how to cope, the stages of grief, and the steps to get through it. Or instead, you go totally numb and distract yourself. That's how I became a workaholic. I avoided my inner turmoil, and work became my primary coping mechanism.

Grief is powerful. If left to its own devices, it can cause significant damage to our inner and outer worlds. We set aside our emotions, thinking we'll deal with them later. But "later" never comes, and avoiding them wreaks havoc on us physically, mentally, emotionally, and spiritually.

You grieve a loved one who passed away. The life you thought that you would live. The career you left behind. The healthy body you once had.

When you see someone take their last breath on this earth, it changes you on the inside. As a live-in caretaker for two of my grandparents, I could see their decline month by month and day after day. Going from a walker, then to a wheelchair, to being 100 percent bedridden. From eating solid foods to only liquids. Going to the bathroom independently to needing to use a bedside commode. From talking and interacting with others to silence. You know what's coming, but nothing prepares you for it.

Have you ever gone through a loss that was so heart-wrenching that you whispered, "I don't know if I can do this," or "I'm not sure how to handle this"?

It brings a heaviness. Some call it depression. Some call it anxiety. No matter how hard you try, you can't escape it. You're hurting so deeply that you don't know what to do. You feel that you can't talk to anyone about it. No one will understand. You don't know how to put what you're feeling into words.

What can we do? Our mind tells us to keep moving. Suck it up, buttercup. Get a grip. You don't have a choice. You must put one foot in front of the other because people are counting on you.

We feel like we don't have time to fall apart, so we lock our feelings in a box, throw away the key, and keep going. But it's exhausting, being strong all the time. We end up putting on fake smiles and saying that we're "fine" so other people don't feel awkward or uncomfortable. But on the inside, we are far from fine.

Over time, we find ourselves getting angry, negative, sad, depressed—maybe all of the above in the span of an hour. Then, out of nowhere, we burst into tears in the grocery store parking lot even though we thought we were "better" or "over it."

Everything makes us upset, even the small things. For example, someone gave us a dirty look, cut us off in traffic, had a certain tone, or talked about us behind our backs. The stress is piling on and results in either overeating or undereating, sleep issues, anxiety, depression, headaches, stomach issues, and so much more. It's too much for one person to deal with, and we often feel like we are going out of our minds.

That inner stuff we have yet to deal with boils to the surface. Dealing with it later, stuffing it down, searching articles, crying in the shower—nothing is helping! So how do we handle this?

First and foremost, grief is a personal and private journey. No one grieves the same way. There is no magic timetable. There is no secret answer. All of your emotions are normal, even the negative ones.

Grief is universal yet unique to the individual.

Wherever you are in your journey with grief and loss, you are not alone. No matter the circumstances, God is with you. I am with you.

I learned that grief is a process through the losses in my career, health, finances, relationships, and the passing away of loved ones, friends, and co-workers. There are many complexities and layers. I'm still dealing with some of it, but the goal is to share with you some stories and tools I've learned through personal experience and as a certified grief coach.

In the pages of this book, we'll focus on the real and raw aspects of grief. We'll explore the questions we all think about but never say out loud:

- How can I make space to grieve when I have too much to do?
- Am I less of a Christian because I feel angry?
- How do I do this when I need to be strong for others?
- Why do I get annoyed when people mean well but offer stereotypical clichés like, "Sorry for your loss"?
- How do I share my grief without being seen as a negative person?

- Does this type of sadness have an expiration date?
- Where is God? Why did He allow this to happen?
- How do I connect with others when I'm going through so much? Is it okay to be alone?
- And how do I create boundaries and ask for what I need during this process?

Here's a quick snapshot of what we're going to chat about.

When dealing with grief and loss, there comes a point in time when you need to let your guard down. You want to create a safe space to sit with your thoughts and fully feel your emotional pain instead of avoiding, resisting, or hiding from it.

Here's the deal. I don't want you to cope. Let's go beyond that place of just barely surviving and hanging on. That means less Google and more God. I'm guilty of going to Google for information before going to my Bible. We can access so much information at our fingertips, yet we are in constant pain. Is all this information helping or hurting? That's a side question to ponder.

My point is that we have to get beyond the stereotypical advice. Let's face it: grief is an uncomfortable topic for most people. It doesn't matter if you are grieving or want to support someone going through it; there is this I-don't-know-what-to-do-or-say vibe on all sides. This book will shine a light on those moments and provide practical tips for handling those situations when they pop up.

Next, we'll discover how to surrender one's suffering to God. Now, if you rolled your eyes a bit when you read that, I get it. But "surrender" is one of those overused words. That's why we'll break this down in a precise step-by-step process, and you'll learn the secret to making it work so you can experience some relief from your heartache.

But what if you are having a crisis of faith? What if you are questioning God? Congratulations! You're not alone. Asking, "Why, God?" is typical. And when we experience the sudden loss of someone close to us, there are often things we didn't get a chance to say before they went. This can mess with our minds. That's why we'll look at how to release any unresolved anger, confusion, and resentment that tends to crop up when someone we love dies, or when we experience a loss.

Have you noticed that something triggers you and pulls you back into that pit of darkness right when you feel like you are returning to some semblance of "normal"? You feel like you took five steps forward, only to be knocked ten backward. Grief, loss, and pain take us down a road with many twists and turns. So what do we do in those moments? We'll discuss a simple secret that will comfort you when you feel empty, sad, and overwhelmed.

We'll also look at how to involve other people in the process. For instance, do you allow people to support you when handling these challenging times? Do you open up and talk to people? Or do you tend to figure it out on your own and keep quiet? There is no right or wrong answer here. You have to do what's best for you. You don't want to vent to just anyone who will listen, so how can you be selective? Conversely, you want to develop the courage and confidence to be more vulnerable with others instead of suffering in silence. Whatever your natural tendency is, this book is going to challenge us (me included) to bring balance to this part of our journey.

We're all in different stages of the grief journey, so take what you need now and leave the rest for later. May these pages create a deeply emotional experience that supports your grief and leaves you with an inner spirit, knowing that God is with you through all seasons of life.

CHAPTER 1

One More Time

People want to help when they realize that you're grieving. They want to provide comfort, whether through flowers, hugs, sympathy cards, or enough fried chicken and casseroles to feed an army. And they offer words of comfort—but are they really that comforting?

"I'm sorry for your loss" is a nice and well-meaning sentiment, but it does nothing to comfort you. After a while, these social niceties start getting on your nerves. It's like the sound of nails scraping and screeching on a chalkboard. It brings you to the edge. You feel like you might scream if someone says that one more time.

Let's look at a few popular phrases. Have people ever said these to you?

- "Sorry for your loss."
- "Time heals all wounds."
- "They are in a better place now."
- "They lived a good life, right?"
- "This too shall pass."

- "You have to be strong for (fill in the blank)."
- "How are you coping?"
- "You've got to get ahold of yourself."
- "Life goes on."
- "You should be over this by now."
- "No sense in dwelling in the past."
- "It's a blessing in disguise."
- "It was God's will."
- "All you have to do is keep busy."
- "Everything happens for a reason."
- "If you need anything, call me."

These are some of the typical questions and phrases that people say when a loved one dies. But you also hear these phrases when going through other types of losses.

"Sorry you lost your job." "Sorry your relationship didn't work out, but maybe it's for the best." "You'll find a better job." "You'll beat that disease." "It's a blessing in disguise."

Here's the truth: there is nothing anyone can say or do that will 100 percent make the pain stop. But that doesn't mean people won't try. And some days, all you want to do is crawl into a deep, dark, hole and avoid everyone.

On some level, you know that things get easier with time. The intensity lessens, and hopefully, you'll find your footing again. But emotionally, you aren't ready to hear this, especially not when a loss is recent.

The reality is that grief makes most people shift and squirm in their seats. If you are grieving, you feel like you have to hold it all together. You have to manage your emotions and be strong for others. You may even feel ashamed and guilty for getting so annoyed with people, even when you know they mean well. It's a constant cycle that leaves you emotionally exhausted.

I remember when people would come over to visit my grandfather. They would leave and say, "He's lived a good life." Ummm, yes, he has. Then I would close the door and roll my eyes. Because why in the world is this person giving me a eulogy when my grandfather is still alive in the next room?

On the one hand, I get it. My grandparents went from seeing doctors to palliative care, quickly transitioning to in-home hospice. In-home hospice is when a nurse visits your house to check on the patient once weekly, or more often if needed. A nurse's aide might come to the house to assist or bathe the patient. It's all about managing the symptoms and ensuring they are not in pain. There is no more treatment to be had. It's just about making them as comfortable as possible.

In these situations, everyone starts grieving early. This is often called anticipatory grief. But even under these circumstances, the last thing I wanted to hear was that my grandfather lived a good life while he was still alive in the next room. When you are an exhausted caregiver, those words aren't helpful. Instead, they are downright infuriating.

At that moment, I was mad, but over the years, I realized something. People do not know what to do or say when someone is grieving. We don't learn how to deal with grief. We emulate what other people did when they lost something or someone. We take that information and apply it to our circumstances the best we know how. We stumble, fall on our faces, and try to find our way.

The same is true for those who are grieving. We learned how to react based on what we saw from those around us. Whether that was running away, avoiding, numbing out, or completely falling apart. Because grief is so hard hitting, very few of us had terrific examples of people who knew how to handle grief positively.

Regardless, there can be a level of uncertainty from all sides. So let's dive into this more and look at how you can handle the clichés thrown around when you're grieving or what to do when supporting someone going through it.

When you are the one grieving, here are five things to remember that will help you navigate the stereotypical advice, social awkwardness, and fake smiles.

- **Be honest with where you are at in your journey.** If you avoid or hide your grief, it's possible to do more damage to yourself and others. Putting yourself on the back burner may feel like the best route because of life's constant demands; however, it will catch up to you in the long run. Honor your feelings because they are like a security system alerting you to what's happening inside. It matters.

- **Communicate courageously.** When you are going through a loss, communicating seems like extra work. Why should you make an effort? You're the one who is hurting. But let's be honest. People can't read minds, so don't expect them to pick up on any subtle (or not-so-subtle) cues that you might need space, or that you need to get out of the house for a while. It's best to be up front to avoid unnecessary conflict. Be courageous and ask for what you need because that's showing compassion to those around you, and to yourself.

- **Bring balance with boundaries.** Here's another not-so-pleasant B-word: boundaries. Some people love them, and others don't. This point goes hand in hand with the first two bullet points. You may need to set up some boundaries, especially in the beginning. It's important to realize that needing time for yourself is not selfish. It's okay to say, "No, thank you," when invited somewhere. It's okay to request some alone time. Creating boundaries, setting limits, and communicating your needs to those you trust illustrate a Godly sense of maturity and strength.

- **Focus on the sentiment, not the sentence.** We don't learn how to grieve in school or get a "how-to" manual at church. When someone is grieving, everyone feels like they're walking on eggshells. If you are grieving, you want to be polite and not make anyone uncomfortable. On the flip side, those supporting you don't want to seem trite or uncaring. They want to comfort and lift your spirits, not annoy or anger you. It can be hard to look past the words that well-wishers say, but in most cases, it all comes from a place of kindness. Of course, there can be some exceptions to the rule, but generally, most people want to help. In these moments, it's important to remember we are all doing our best when tragedy strikes. Give yourself grace and consider extending that same grace to others.

- **Go to God more than Google.** In the Bible, David was a king. He carried the weight of an entire nation on his shoulders. He wrestled with his feelings and continuously laid his heart out before God. It's written all through the book of Psalms. He was angry, tormented, depressed, overwhelmed, and remorseful. No matter what he was facing, he talked to God. When we go through a loss, we want information from the why or the "how-to." With convenient access at our fingertips, we can turn to a search engine for every question that pops into our heads. Let me ask you, where do you turn first, Google or God? It can be easier to type in a problem than go through the Bible and find something that applies to your situation. Here are some tips to change that: 1) Find comfort in familiar favorites by reading your favorite scripture or story. 2) Go to an all-encompassing verse that you can use when your stress is getting the best of you. Memorize it, and write it on a Post-it note or index card to connect with God in your moment of need. Have this prepared in advance so that you don't have to search for encouragement when you are struggling. And if the Bible isn't your cup of tea, find a quote or song lyric that speaks to you. Music is often my go-to because it can touch places in my heart and soul that text can't reach.

It's easy to try to handle everything yourself in times of grief. You may feel like you have to be strong for others. You may feel like you want to be left alone. You may immediately be open to talking with a coach or counselor. You may need to phone a friend and vent regularly. Journaling in silence may be your go-to way to process. Whatever it is, know that you are not alone. Remember that God is your source and strength when you have questions circling in your mind and don't know what to do next.

Let's flip the script briefly and look at the other side. When you support a grieving person, here are five ways to be present as they go through a significant life change or loss.

- **Acknowledge their pain.** When someone is going through a loss, we often tiptoe around it. We avoid saying the person's name, especially when a loved one has passed away. It's crucial to bring validity to their pain by acknowledging it and the person. We can do this by simply saying, "That sucks," or "I can't begin to imagine how you are feeling," or "I love you, and I'm here for you." You can even share a story. You can say, "I have a memory of (state their loved one's name); may I share it with you now?" Asking their permission shows you are being respectful of where they are at in the present moment. If they agree, share away. And if they don't, say that you'd be happy to share it later if and when they are ready. These examples acknowledge their pain and where they are in the process. If we don't create space for someone grieving, they will most likely suppress their emotions because they don't feel free to open up.

- **Let them get it out.** Grieving is a roller-coaster ride of emotions. Let them tap into all of the twists and turns without any censorship. Let them vent, yell, cry, or escape for a few minutes. Do they need to scream into a pillow? Do they need to find a punching bag and whale on it with a jab-cross-punch combination? Sometimes those who are grieving hold things inside because they don't want to make others uncomfortable. Allowing them space to feel their feelings is truly a gift. Be present with them in their pain. Of course, the caveat is as long as it doesn't hurt them or others.

- **Be okay with where they are in the process.** It's hard enough dealing with the loss itself, but to feel judgment on top of that adds a type of stress that no one needs. Try to avoid pushing your agenda. For example, you may want the person grieving to talk to a counselor or go to a grief support group. Those are valid suggestions, but perhaps wait until they have had some time to sit with their emotions or bring it up themself. After all, they are just trying to get through the next hour, not thinking about the rest of their life. If you feel they are "stuck," you could bring it up gently down the road. And if you do, it's best to position it as an open-ended question. For example, "I can't imagine how you feel or what you're going through. Would you ever consider talking with a grief specialist if or when you are ready?"

- **Create a safe space for them to share.** Recognize that grief is different for each person. What works for one person won't necessarily work for another. You may know what it's like to lose something or someone. That means you can relate. You know what loss feels like, but don't pretend you know exactly what they went through and how they feel and think. In these moments, it's a time to listen more than speak. Skip the temptation to insert your opinion or tell them how they "should" be behaving or grieving. Instead, your goal is to be present and create a safe space where they can talk openly.

- **Check in and follow up with them regularly.** Life happens, and we all get busy. But if we genuinely want to be there for our family and friends, it will take some effort. For example, think beyond the funeral when it comes to grief. Key dates, like birthdays and anniversaries, can be emotional triggers, so reach out regularly. The key word here is regularly. Write a note, put a reminder alert on your phone, or whatever your preferred system is, to remind yourself to check in with people occasionally. They may want to talk, or they may want to be alone. Either way, respect their response and rest assured they are grateful for your kindness.

We need to honor each other in moments of grief and loss. We must move away from trying to "fix" the person or issue and shift to a place where we are fully present, ready to listen, and have a servant's heart for those experiencing grief.

This chapter highlights how we perceive grief, especially in social settings. It permits grievers to feel annoyed and angry with the bombardment of clichés when a loss occurs.

We must also remind both our hearts and minds that we don't know how to grieve or what to say when someone is suffering. Like most of life, it's a live-and-learn process. It's even more important, because of this, to remember that every person and situation is different. Let's consider, meditate on, and write down answers to the following questions before we dive into the next chapter and examine how we cope with grief:

- What would happen if we let people off the hook in moments of high stress?
- What if every emotion is Godly, even the negative ones?
- What would happen if we approached fragile hearts with a tenderness that seems missing in this fast-paced world that is continuously "go, go, go" and "do, do, do"?
- What if we slowed down and let God get involved in our grief?

CHAPTER 2

Frame of Mind

A lthough we repeatedly hear certain phrases when we are going through a loss, we understand that most people's intentions are good. They want to support you and be there for you. They just have not been taught how. But we also have some ingrained beliefs about grief that we've often learned from our culture, family, Google, and society. So it's time to turn inward; the next few chapters will look at how we process our pain mentally, emotionally, physically, and spiritually. We'll discover that grief doesn't impact one or two areas of our lives. Instead, it's a multi-level disruptor.

The Stages

So what's one of the most common beliefs about grief? It's about the actual process itself: the five stages of grief. You've probably heard about these ever-popular steps through pamphlets, books, family members, or even from your online searches. But, for the fun of it, let's briefly recap them.

Elizabeth Kübler-Ross, a Swiss-American psychiatrist, developed the five stages of grief in 1969. These five stages include denial, anger, bargaining, depression, and acceptance. Let's break each one down:

- **Denial** is living your life as if nothing has changed. It's ignoring the loss and treating it as if it never happened in the first place. This stage is full-on pretending you're fine as if nothing happened. In this stage, denial is a mask of self-protection and impacts your mental well-being.

- **Anger** is an emotional response to what's going on in your world. And it can take many forms. Someone can get angry and ask questions like, "Why is this happening to me?" This person may be defensive, argumentative, and gearing up for a fight. They may talk about getting even, revenge, or legal action. They might blame God or others for the tragedy. In this stage, it's all about defending one's self.

- **Bargaining** is all about negotiations, both big and small. It's about making deals with God or others to change the current chaotic circumstances. For example, someone might say, "God, if you heal her, I'll go to church weekly for the rest of my life." Or if your relationship is falling apart, someone might say, "If you'll stay and we don't get divorced, I'll go to counseling." It's a transactional exchange.

- **Depression** can involve hard-core feelings of hopelessness and sadness and can even include isolating yourself from others. It's a feeling of being discouraged and down-hearted because of the emotional trauma. There is a heaviness associated with depression that feels almost as if you are suffocating from all the overwhelming thoughts and feelings of grief. Many people who are depressed often wear a mask because of the social stigma around it.

- **Acceptance** is the final stage of this process. It's admitting your reality. That what you're going through is happening. Some even say that this stage can help someone find comfort and peace.

These five stages are popular and, at times, overused on the topic of grief and loss. To me, these stereotypical stages feel like an overly clinical to-do list that you check off to ensure you're grieving in healthy ways. The bottom line is that grief is not a linear process. And while I don't think that was the author's original intent when she developed the five stages, it's one way that many people view this topic. You can go through these stages over time or in one day or even in the course of an hour, which I can vouch for from personal experience!

Generally, most people go through these stages in some form or fashion. But I wouldn't put them in any order or say that everyone experiences all of them. Everyone is unique, and people can also change how they grieve depending on where they are in life. For instance, I mourned my great-grandmother's death when I was fifteen much differently than when my grandfather passed away after being one of his live-in caregivers at thirty-seven. The five stages of grief and other similar advice often oversimplify this complicated issue.

By the way, Elizabeth Kübler-Ross later added a few additional stages to this process. The seven stages of grief include:

- Shock and denial
- Pain and guilt
- Anger and bargaining
- Depression
- The upward turn
- Reconstruction and working through
- Acceptance and hope

Please remember that only some things you read about the subject will be true for your situation. Here's an example:

I read a cringe-worthy question when doing some research for this book. The question asked, "What stage of grief happens when you cry?" And I was taken aback by the response. The reply was, "The depression stage of grief because that's when you are sad." I sat there for a minute, reading that line over and over again. Then I got annoyed. What kind of answer is that? You can cry at any or all stages! This is why I think that the five-stage model is so limiting.

Let's follow this line of thought. For example, have you ever been so angry that you cried? I did this in a professional setting once, which only added fuel to my emotional fire. I was so mad at this man's request. It was unreasonable based on everything I had on my plate. Usually, I negotiate and say, "I can get that done if I can push this other project's deadline out." But that wasn't an option in this case.

So I explained my point of view (calmly and rationally while boiling under the surface), and then it happened. Suddenly, those warm, salty tears started to trickle down my face. My entire being was conflicted because I was forcing my body and words to remain calm when I wanted to give this person a piece of my mind. Because of that internal struggle, tears came out of my baby-blue eyes. Next, I had to excuse myself to the bathroom, which made me even more furious—beating myself up as my high-heeled shoes went clickety-clack down the hall. *How could I let them see me cry? And at work of all places.* This was yet another condescending jerk who thought that women are emotional, and in that conference room, I felt I proved that outdated adage right.

But the truth is, I wasn't being overly emotional. I wasn't depressed or sad. I was so angry that I was trying not to curse, yell, or slap someone. It was humiliating. But that's an example of how anger can lead us to tears. So to say that you only cry when you are sad or depressed is complete nonsense. You may have an example or two about how this statement is false based on your *own* experiences.

That story illustrates that sometimes when you read things, you may need to take it with a grain of salt and ignore it. Remember, we all connect with things differently. So here's the deal: if the five (or seven) stages of grief resonate with where you are in your journey, that's great. If not, that's cool too. The goal is to find tools that will help you on your journey.

Do-it-Yourself Model

When you know how to grieve or follow the socially acceptable clichés, it's easy to think that you can handle it all alone. You manage all the moving pieces in your life; why not this? After all, you're already a professional juggler. But what happens when you have more disappointing news on top of what you are already dealing with in your life? The grief starts to stack up. The pain increases and becomes overwhelming with every compounding blow. Sooner or later, something's got to give.

I used to think that I could handle everything by myself. I could function and do life, business as usual, while secretly dealing with my heartache. Here's how it happened. Once upon a time, I was grieving my first love, the man I thought I would marry. Then two months later, I was in a car accident that totaled my car and messed up my neck and lower back. It felt like my world was caving in all around me. It impacted me emotionally, mentally, physically, and spiritually. Plus, it left me with many doubts and questions about my faith and life.

When losses happen, life can pile up. When it piles up, we push it to the side, shove our emotions down, and keep on keepin' on. But what happens when we step back and see our behavior from the outside looking in? Keeping ourselves distracted and stuffing down our emotions is a recipe for disaster. We may find ourselves verbally vomiting all over an innocent person or taking it out on the ones we love the most.

That's why we must understand how we deal with our challenges and recognize our triggers. How do our bodies, minds, and spirits respond? Everything is connected. We cannot separate parts of ourselves. To address the whole, we must look at the multiple areas we are affected by trauma. First up, let's look at mental well-being.

Mental Well-Being

There are many different definitions of mental health and well-being. This popular topic covers anything, such as our concentration, productivity, stress management, and mental illness. On top of that, the words "mental and emotional health" are seemingly interchangeable. But for this book, mental health will refer to how you *think* and *function* while processing information about your loss. Emotional health is how you *feel* about and *react* to that information.

Our brains are fascinating. They have the capacity for greatness. We put it through the wringer, yet it can alter, evolve, and heal (especially if we are willing). Our brains follow our lead and respond to what we repeatedly tell them, and from there, behaviors and patterns form. Scientifically, this is called neuroplasticity.

So if we are grieving a loss and have continuous thoughts that stress and overwhelm us, it can be like a horrible song that never stops playing in our minds. What happens is that when we go through a painful situation, our mind senses that we are tense and on edge. Our brain (amygdala) rushes to the rescue by triggering our fight-or-flight response. We build up defenses, or we run for the hills. Either way, it's all done in the name of self-preservation.

When you are grieving, neurochemicals and hormones flood your brain. When this happens, it can disrupt our ability to think straight and focus, impacting our sleep, appetite, and much more. We'll dive into how grief affects our physical bodies in Chapter 4. For now, I want to highlight how heartache, loss, and pain can impact our overall productivity.

Have you ever had a significant loss and felt completely out of it? You need help to think straight, usually in the form of caffeine. When people are talking, you tend to lose track of the conversation. And when you do respond, you lose your train of thought. It boils down to this: processing information is hard when you are grieving, and this is a common struggle.

We live in a crazy and unfair world. We can easily get disoriented and flustered because of all the information that we consume, not to mention all the things we must do, such as funeral arrangements and financial audits. And so our entire being gets overloaded, leaving us craving a time-out.

But this doesn't mean that we can't function. On the contrary, many of us have to keep going for the sake of others. And sometimes that's easier because that means we don't have time to grieve. But that doesn't mean we are giving our best. Typically, it means that we are getting by and surviving, which looks different for each of us.

At work or in social settings, we may feel scatterbrained. We aren't present in meetings. We half answer questions. Our responses may be similar to:

- "Huh?"
- "Wait, what?"
- "What did you say? I missed that."
- "I completely forgot about that."
- "I'm so sorry. Can you repeat that?"

And then we feel upset, and as if we do not measure up. That, somehow, we are failing at life while our world is crumbling down around our feet. Have you ever wondered if you are failing at this whole grieving thing too? I know I did, as if that's even a thing. But grief can shake one's confidence so much that we sometimes feel embarrassed and a little stupid.

At some point, your brain shuts off and doesn't want to focus or concentrate on anything. It's working too hard to process what's happening in your life. So what's the solution?

The problem is that you cannot solve grief. It's not a mathematical equation. It's different for each person. And it can change depending on the type of loss, our age, support system, and many other factors. But when talking about our mental well-being during grief, one of my top recommendations is journaling.

At the end of Chapter 1, I asked you to think through and write out answers to a few questions. You'll continue to see that throughout the book. That's why I want to take a moment to talk about journaling. It's often a go-to grief tool mentioned in all the books and blogs, as well as by counselors. So why is it such a big deal? I want to talk about that here because it relates to our topic of mental well-being.

In full transparency, I don't always journal. When I do, it's because I'm emotionally struggling and can't clear my mind. It's like a record playing repeatedly in your head that won't go away no matter how hard you try to shut it off. Stuffing down my emotions works for a while, and then I get snippy and snappy with everyone. So when the moodiness comes on strong, I know I need to sit down and write it out. But it was a challenging habit for me. I was never a "Dear Diary" type. It didn't feel very productive until I learned more about the science behind it.

Fun fact: I geek out on health hacks and how things work. I want to know the why and any how-to shortcuts so I am efficient with my time. Sounds like a tall order? Sure! But it's possible. I'll share some of the hacks that work for me in a minute, but first, let's look at the benefits of this seemingly commonly referenced technique.

Hands up if you are over every book and blog post recommending that you journal. You're in the right place because I feel the same way. It's everywhere. I don't have the patience, time, or energy to journal for hours. Or to write out every teeny-tiny detail of my day. And what if you live with nosy people? You don't want people all up in your private business!

There are numerous studies on the topic of journaling. Some of the well-known benefits include:

- Journaling is known to help unlock our emotions and improve mental health.
- It's a safe and confidential way of expressing emotion. If you've got nosy people that live with you, it's still doable.
- It provides a deeper level of self-awareness.
- It's an acknowledgment of what's occurring in your life at the time. Documenting what's going on in your life can give you greater insight and wisdom later. If you go back and reread it a year later, you can see how far you've come.
- Journaling can help you clarify beliefs, see thought patterns, and more. It can help you determine why you think and feel like you do.

Journaling our innermost emotions and thoughts when it comes to grief, loss, and trauma is often referred to as expressive writing. It's a way to process difficult seasons in our lives. It lets us get out the thoughts swirling around in our heads and onto paper. Ultimately, journaling allows us an opportunity to remove our masks, even if it's only for a portion of the day.

Throughout this book, questions will gently prompt and nudge you down the path of reflection.

Now you may be wondering, what format of journaling is best? Answer: the one you'll stick with consistently. I journal two times a week.

There are many ways you can start your journaling practice. You can kick it old school with pen and paper. That's my preference. Or you can type notes into your preferred electronic device or even do voice memos on your phone. And if you don't like typing, you can always download a voice-to-text app. Pick the best format for you, or create a new system for your lifestyle.

Expressive writing is a journaling technique often associated with grief and loss because we are diving into our innermost emotions and thoughts. Many books and counselors lean toward expressive writing as the preferred style.

Here are my go-to journaling methods, so you can see how I use them and adapt them to whatever works for you.

"Dear Diary" Method: This is long-form writing. It's when you write out every word you think and feel. It has more sentence structure and paragraphs. You write until you have nothing else to say.

The Bullet Method: This style is quick and great if you are short on time. It's simply a quick, bulleted list of anything on your mind. Think of it like writing a grocery list.

Thought Extension Method: This style resembles a brainstorming session or mind map. Write out bullet points on your day and how you are feeling. As you journal, you may have an additional idea that comes to mind. It's an extension of one of your bullet points. So, draw an arrow from that bullet and keep writing the thoughts that come to mind. It reminds me of the thought bubbles you see in cartoons.

But ultimately, pick what works best for you and your schedule. For example, do a quick entry if you only have five minutes. If you have more time, then do a longhand method. Try not to censor yourself or judge your writing in any way. It's personal and private, meant for your eyes only. It's a time to let it all out, which is unbelievably cathartic.

Note: If you see continual patterns of dark and suicidal thoughts in your writing, you may want to see a professional counselor. This may mean you need extra support to process your thoughts and feelings. One free resource available in the United States is the 988 Suicide & Crisis Lifeline (formerly the National Suicide Prevention Lifeline 1-800-273-TALK). Check out their website at https://988lifeline.org/ to chat with someone or call/text 988 on your phone.

As you go through this process, the secret is to be like George. Remember him? He's a fun-loving character living in popular children's books—a curious little monkey who goes on adventures and loves to explore.

I invite you to become curious about your grief and how it's showing up in your life. We need to take time to reflect and process what's going on. It won't be easy. It will be brutal at times. But getting in this frame of mind is the foundation of your journey.

If you picked up this book, you might be struggling with your emotions, whether your loss is recent or happened years ago. So, take your time with this book. Many chapters contain thought-provoking questions. Think through each one carefully and go at your own pace.

No matter where you are in the grief cycle, I hope you remain curious and open. Stick with it even if something doesn't resonate with you right away. It will make a huge difference as you walk through this challenging season.

I'm still learning from my different experiences with grief. Caregiving for my elderly grandparents taught me a lot, and processing it took me a while. Initially, I needed to take care of my physical body and catch up on rest. That meant ignoring the emotional side of things for a time. I didn't want to think about anything else because that might risk opening the emotional floodgates. But after the house was sold and we were back home, I turned inward. There is a time and place for all aspects of grief.

Grief is powerful. It can keep us stuck or evolve and add something unexpected to our lives. My invitation is simple; when you're ready to dive in, channel George and get curious.

CHAPTER 3

Little White Lies

After a loss, have you ever asked yourself: Who am I? What do I do now? Where do I go from here? These are common questions we ask ourselves when significant life changes and major stressors occur. And grief certainly qualifies!

Typically, grievers move forward in their day-to-day lives. But many do so wearing masks. We wear a mask at work so we can pay the bills. We conceal our feelings from our families to be strong for them. We pretend we're fine with friends, accessorizing with cute shoes and fake smiles.

So we question everything—from who we are to our beliefs to our purpose on Earth. We debate if we are in the "right" careers and relationships. And most of us don't want to bring others down, so instead, we bottle up our emotions. We put them on a shelf and tell ourselves that we'll deal with it later. But the masks, the fake smiles, and "I'm fine" replies are little white lies we tell ourselves so we can function. These self-protecting tactics can work for a short time and, truth be told, are sometimes needed; however, they eventually catch up to us in the end.

Do you ever feel like there is something unsettled on the inside of you? It's an internal battle or, rather, a conflict between what you are saying and feeling, which can lead to bigger issues down the road. It's a recipe for disease that can impact your entire well-being. This is called being out of alignment.

To get back on track, sometimes we need an adjustment. For example, when you are out of alignment physically, you might go to a chiropractor to get a spinal adjustment. The process can sometimes be painful. Afterward, we might feel sore and achy. But once those symptoms subside, we end up feeling better. It's the same for the grieving process.

It can be easy to put on a show when we are grieving. We try to be what others think we should be after a loss. We try to do all the "right" things. This type of people-pleasing behavior can leave you confused and exhausted. But you have to find your path. You have to grieve in a way that feels right for you.

The fact is, it's easy to lose your identity in grief. For example, in the Bible (Ruth 1), there was a woman named Naomi. First, her husband died, then ten years later, her two sons died. She was consumed by grief, so much so that she changed her name to Mara. The meaning of Naomi is "pleasant," and the name Mara means "bitter." It seems dramatic; however, in those times, the definition of one's name said more about you than a full-scope biography.

Grief can swallow you up, leaving you empty, confused, and overwhelmed. We tell ourselves and others that we are "fine" and "dealing with it," but we don't know how to take the next best step. Perhaps we are scared to allow ourselves to feel or share our pain. These deceptive little white lies are like a warm security blanket. And this bubble of perceived safety is a common avoidance tactic, especially in social settings.

Have you been advised about how to grieve? Perhaps someone said to embrace every emotion. I encourage that; however, there is also a time and place. Grief unfolds differently for each of us. You may be in a situation where you need to bottle up those emotions for a short period. That's okay. Just remember that at some point, you have to take that key out and unlock the contents. What are you going to find? When I did that, here's what I discovered.

Work Was My Worth

Work has always been part of my identity, and I take pride in my work ethic. But the reality was, work both aided me and stopped me from taking a hard look in the mirror.

When you start work at thirteen, you grow up fast. And God graciously sent opportunities my way at a young age. So I dove in. The atta-girl pat on the back for being accurate and fast with my work only fueled my ambition. I was goal-oriented and didn't want to stop growing. I kept achieving and climbing the ladder. But by the time that I was in my early thirties, I was overworked, stressed, and burned out. A car accident in 2006 left me with chronic pain and migraines. I spent years in pain and working long hours. Everything was catching up to me at once. One morning, I woke up with chest pains. It was a minor scare; however, I knew a change was needed. It was a difficult decision, but I left my career in 2015. It was like an extended vacation at first. I caught up on rest and did my own thing. But then, I hit a wall. I felt inadequate because I didn't have a steady income.

Working was my go-to way of coping when things got messy. I realized how my identity and worth were attached to work. I felt like a fish out of water. Flip-flopping, trying to get myself back to where I thought I belonged.

So, I started unraveling and evaluating my life to create new goals. I had to start somewhere, and it began by getting honest and assessing my inner world.

During that time, I read many books and attended many seminars. But unfortunately, some of these seminars believed that your feelings were irrelevant. You have to suck it up and keep going no matter what happens. Well, that's what got me in trouble in the first place! This line of thinking teaches people to cover up their feelings and mask them.

I believe that God gave us the capacity to feel for a reason. But, admittedly, it can get dangerous, especially when we allow it to consume us to the extent that it becomes our identity and impacts how we live our lives, crippling our ability to take action. Overall, our thoughts and feelings are information. We need to use that information and decide how to proceed.

When talking about action, many of us think twenty-five moves ahead. What we need to focus on is the next best step. One step at a time. When we focus too far in front of us, we get overwhelmed. Here are a few of the steps that we've already covered:

First, give yourself permission to feel all your emotions.

Second, identify your season. What stage of the grieving process are you in? What is the best way to grieve with everything on your plate?

Third, get curious about what you are thinking and feeling. This simple mindset trick will help you navigate your journey to a place of productive hope and healing.

Finally, recognize your behavior patterns, how you are coping, and what you gravitate toward when you're hurting from tragic circumstances.

As you know, I believe in allowing your emotions to happen. But, if you keep them hidden, eventually, it will catch up to you, and not in a good way. The issue is when we think about the negative all the time, which is called negative rumination. I'm all for the whole spectrum of human emotions, but it can become an issue. If you dwell in a place of bitterness, it's easy to get lost.

When my dad's mom passed away, I was in my early twenties. Someone very close to me made me feel as if being sad was ridiculous. They asked, "Didn't she live a good and long life?"

I said, "Well, yes. But she was my grandmother."

I was confused and shocked by the response. It left me a bit speechless. Why was this person making me feel less than because of my emotions? In my opinion, this is a dangerous way to respond to someone who is grieving. Because it can make the person feel like their emotions and thoughts aren't valid. Over time, they may share less and less, not just with that person, but overall.

In the thick of our pain, we don't want to be preached to or have Bible verses shoved in our faces. They are often about: "This too shall pass," "Time heals all wounds," "They are in a better place," "He lived a good life"—all of those things you don't want to hear when you're upset.

The reality is, the person who died is free. Unfortunately, we are the ones that remain and are left to deal with all the broken pieces left behind. It's easy to disconnect and drive others away. It's harder to let people into our pain.

Invalidating our emotions and ignoring them makes us emotionally constipated. So, we need a process to get us flowing again so our internal junk doesn't lead to a meltdown.

The worst thing is to stuff your feelings down or have an I-will-deal-with-it-later mindset, because the fact is you won't. You'll find excuse after excuse. I gotta work, cook, clean the toilet, and do anything to keep busy so I don't have to think. But there comes a time when you must face what you feel. Now that's something I've avoided, and it stole so much. I became more of a people pleaser, the yes-girl. I didn't know who I was. I lost my voice. I lost my identity. I forgot who I was and who God created me to be because I didn't deal with my inner mess.

Surround yourself with people who encourage you when you are struggling instead of dismissing your feelings. When someone you love dies, you feel out of sorts. A piece of you is missing. There is both an internal and external tug-of-war happening. So how do we deal with it all?

Avoiding the Pain of Loss

Sometimes after a loss, we have more responsibilities. For example, our circumstances might require more of us for a season, so we can't focus on our loss. Instead, we need to take care of others or handle financial matters. We keep busy in these moments because we have to keep going. We do what we must to get by, even though we want to hop off this neverending merry-go-round.

In some ways, acknowledging our emotions is too overwhelming for our human circuits. And in other ways, we are stressing out because of the neverending to-do list coupled with the tension we feel because of the storm growing inside us. There always seems to be something that stops us from letting our guard down: fear.

We're afraid that once we start crying, we won't stop. So we avoid, cope, and distract ourselves in any way we can. But escaping our grief can only bring temporary relief, while the consequences of ongoing avoidance can last a lifetime.

Have you ever been in so much pain that you needed it to stop, even just for a few minutes? Instead, you reach for anything that will help numb the pain. You know it doesn't solve anything. You know it's only a temporary fix, but you need your mind and emotions to shut off. You desperately want an escape.

Finding something or someone to help you forget your feelings is easy. Many of us "cope" by using diversions. These diversions can even disguise themselves as things on our to-do lists. This busyness can be anything from running errands, working overtime, social media scrolling, online shopping, cleaning, laundry, carpooling, cooking, or taking care of other members of our family. But these everyday life things need to happen so we can keep functioning, right? It's not like we can drop our daily chores and responsibilities because we are grieving! It's an easy thing to tell ourselves. So we fill our plates and fill up our lists.

And then, when we find a little space in our week, we may find even more distractions such as binge-watching TV, food, sleep, alcohol, exercise, serial dating, sex, sleep, drugs (over the counter, prescription, legal, and illegal), smoking—the list is endless. When we numb our pain with other things or substances, it keeps us from thinking or feeling anything else. We are in survivor mode.

By "we," I mean me. Work was my main go-to. It's how I got by or survived pretty much everything. I tried to handle it myself when I realized I was using work to distract myself from the inner mess. I'm a grown, intelligent woman. But without thinking, I would grab my laptop and start working because I had an idea. Or I needed to research something. Or I saw an email that I needed to answer right then. Then the next thing I knew, three hours would have gone by. I felt like I constantly needed to be *doing* something. I needed to stay busy to distract myself from what I felt inside. But this way of coping was not dealing with the heart of my grief. Being an overachieving professional was a role I played and a mask I wore daily.

These avoidance tactics end up taking a toll on our overall well-being. It's almost as if we are slowly fading when we don't allow room for our thoughts, feelings, and emotions. Instead, we reach for our preferred method of escape because it's easier than reflecting on what's happened in our lives.

Everyone's go-to is different; each person often has multiple coping mechanisms. Even healthy things can be used as a crutch when we struggle with grief. But here is the thing, many of us need to be made aware of what we are doing to get by. There are conscious ways of avoidance, like the typical no-nos or red flags, but there are also those sneaky ones that we don't see. That's why we must reflect on the reasons behind our actions.

Let me ask you, how are you choosing to numb your pain?

I don't love labeling things as good or bad, but it's easier to explain for illustration purposes.

Work is not a "bad" thing. It's a good thing. We need to work to live and pay bills, right? But I used my career as a distraction.

Exercising every day is a great, healthy habit. But if you are doing it to avoid the hard conversations that await you at home, then you are using it as a means of escape.

For some, watching TV is like soothing therapy, but for someone else, it can become an addictive time waster. So we must evaluate how we cope, our methods to avoid stress, and why we are using them.

It comes down to the intention behind the action and the *real* reason behind why we are doing it. It's a form of self-protection. Truly, the battle is in our minds.

And every person who grieves does so differently. So the tools that will work for one person typically won't work for another. That's why this is a process and a journey.

Emulating Your Past

Sometimes to see those signs, we need to look at the past. How did you learn to grieve? It's not taught in schools. You learned from your environment and various types of observation. Who are you emulating? Is it serving you?

What is your reaction to your current circumstances? In the last chapter, you may have recognized how you numb your pain. You may have connected the dots from how you are dealing with your loss to how you've seen others handle it in the past. We often mimic what we know and how we've seen others deal with things from past experiences, often from childhood. Here are some questions to journal and think through as we continue:

- What do you believe about grief?
- How did those around you handle it?
- What did you learn about grieving from them?
- What have your spiritual beliefs, doctrine, and religion taught you about grief?

Tricks When Triggered

I focus on the basics when I find myself triggered by grief. One exercise is to return to the beginning of life: breath. I often need to remember in the busyness of life to take time to focus on how I'm breathing into my body. To fill my lungs with a deep inhale, let it all out with an elongated exhale. I first learned about the importance of breathing through yoga. But over time and through my studies, I see how impactful this is when we connect with our origin.

It's as simple as a deep breath in and out. But, sometimes, I need extra support to get me in the mood so my body and mind relax. So, I set the stage by entering a quiet room, lighting a candle, and focusing my gaze on the flicker of the flame. This process helps me get calm and centered.

Two other options include box breathing and the four-seven-eight breathing technique. I often think about my breathing more at the end of the day, but you can do it any time during your day. Breathing techniques are a great way to calm your body and mind, especially when anxious and spinning out.

Discover Your Distractions

It's a slow fade because sometimes we don't even realize that we are using the busyness of life and other distractions not to feel our pain. We know that we shouldn't put our feelings on the shelf. We know that it's best for us if we face our feelings head-on. But the reality is different. Often, when we reach for our distraction of choice, it's done subconsciously.

And every person who grieves does so differently. It's such a personal journey, which makes it hard to open up to others about it. But you are taking a huge step. We must reach a point where we are consciously aware that we must face our grief. We know our emotions, even those nasty ones, are part of the journey. That acknowledgment is what prepares your heart for what's next.

Find someplace you can go (even if that's locking yourself in the bathroom) to think and feel through the following questions:

- How can I make space to grieve when I have too much to do?
- Am I less of a Christian because I feel angry?
- How do I process everything when I need to be strong for others?
- How does losing a loved one affect your mental health?
- How does unresolved grief affect mental health?
- What happens to your brain when you are grieving?

- What emotions have you felt through this painful time?
- How do you handle your day-to-day responsibilities when you are suffering internally?
- Are you using the busyness of life as an escape?
- How are you choosing to numb your pain?

Writing the answers on paper can help you unravel the emotions that you've stuffed down. In addition, referencing these answers as we progress on this journey can be revealing. Even if you are not ready to think about these questions, let alone answer them. Try this simple step: write the question in your journal and walk away. The answers will come.

Overall, you want to:

1. Become aware of your habits.
2. Accept where you are right now.
3. Evaluate your coping mechanisms and determine what's beneficial and what leaves you feeling empty.

A few examples are binge-watching TV, under- or overeating, sleeping, exercising, alcohol, drugs (over the counter to prescription to illegal), sex, shopping, smoking, and work. But there are many others.

It's your turn. What are you using to numb your emotions, thoughts, or pain? What are you doing to avoid and distract yourself? Is fear holding you back from grieving? What's standing in your way?

Grief impacts us in multiple dimensions. So get curious about yourself and how you deal with the hard stuff.

CHAPTER 4

Collision Course

Have you ever gone through a loss and then experienced physical symptoms in your body? Continually struggling with your circumstances' emotions and thoughts can impact your body. It's true: being sick with grief is a real thing.

Our emotions, thoughts, and feelings greatly impact our bodies. You can feel your stomach tighten at a funeral. You feel hot and sweaty before giving a presentation. You might feel anxious when you lose a job or financial security. When these things happen, they can impact you on many different levels.

I didn't understand this fully until 2016. Seeing my grandmother take her last breath changed me. The months leading up to it were difficult. I was one of her live-in caretakers. She transitioned from going to the doctor to palliative care to in-home hospice. Three months after this transition, family members walked the halls of my grandparents' home all night and into the morning. We took turns giving her medication, taking naps, and downing coffee. There were tear-stained faces exchanging worried looks in passing, and moments of not knowing what to do or say. But we all anticipated and knew what was coming next. When she took her last breath, we gathered around her hospital-like bed that now occupied the back bedroom. As everyone said their goodbyes, I whispered in her ear that I loved her and would see her again soon.

Fast-forwarding eight months later, I was hospitalized the week after Father's Day in 2017. I was sick, could barely walk without help, and my body was rebelling. Lying on the uncomfortable hospital bed, I remembered the words I had spoken to my grandmother. They echoed in my mind over and over again. I panicked and told God my words to my grandmother weren't literal. I didn't mean it quite this soon. It's not my time yet, because there were things I still wanted to do on this side of life.

I didn't know what was going on with my body. The doctors told me I had an autoimmune disease, but I was in denial. I didn't want to accept this as a fact. But eventually, I realized that my way of dealing with issues was not working.

My health issues weren't from one singular experience. It was from the ongoing stress that I had experienced over the years. My it's-not-a-big-deal and push-through-it mentality caught up with me big time. Keeping busy and working too much could no longer be my go-to coping method.

Over time, I discovered many layers of grief. I worked with coaches and counselors. I was praying, reading devotions, and doing all the "right" Bible-believing things. But I still carried this heaviness; something felt physically and emotionally broken. All of my physical, mental, emotional, and spiritual stuff collided. There were things I continually brushed aside because what's the point in dwelling on them? After all, I learned to keep on keepin' on, because those adult responsibilities don't vanish when life takes unexpected twists and turns. We can't quit life because it gets complicated.

Have you ever connected your physical symptoms to what's happening in your inner world? Let's take some time to look at why that happens and what to watch out for. The consequences of not dealing with your emotions could be severe.

What do we need to look for when going through life and loss? How do we make the connection between our inner and outer worlds?

When we have negative emotions and thoughts, it kicks off a biochemical response in our bodies. If we experience something like the end of a relationship, the death of a loved one, or losing a job, we attach emotion or a feeling to that circumstance. That information and response are recorded and stored in our bodies.

Think about how your body reacts when you recall a traumatic event. What's your body doing as you remember the people there, where you were, and how you felt? What did you see, smell, hear, taste, or touch? As you remember, you might start to feel anxious, angry, or sad. That's because it's all connected to the neural psychosomatic network in our brains.

I'll spare you the biology lesson, but realizing that our body remembers these things is essential, especially if we don't heal or process grief and pain. It feels like our sorrow is multiplying, which can quickly overwhelm us to the point where our emotions spiral and our physical bodies go haywire.

Let's break down the common symptoms so you can keep an eye out for them if bad news comes and stress skyrockets:

- Depression
- Phobias
- Panic attacks
- Fatigue
- Exhaustion
- Insomnia
- Anxiety
- Confusion
- Forgetfulness
- Lack of focus
- Headaches/migraines

Chronic or ongoing stress can start to impact different areas in your body, such as the heart, immune system, and digestive systems. Here are just a few things that can happen:

- High blood pressure
- Chest pains and spasms
- Heart attacks, strokes, aneurysms
- Colds/infections
- Autoimmune disorders, including rheumatoid arthritis, Crohn's, Hashimoto's, ulcerative colitis, Lyme disease, etc.
- Changes in appetite
- Constipation
- Diarrhea
- Nausea and vomiting
- Cramping
- Ulcers
- Leaky gut/IBS

Have you ever dealt with anything from these two lists? If so, it can impact your life in many ways, including your home and work productivity. We must know how these things are connected because they can make a huge difference in our lives.

When drowning in what's happening around us, we must take care of ourselves. It's easier said than done, though. There may be too much to do when going through a loss. There could be funeral preparations and travel arrangements when a death occurs. With the end of a relationship, you may need to find a new place to live or juggle schedules if children are involved. We may want to hide or collapse from the pain, but life keeps spinning.

What does the Bible say about it all?

In the Bible, Job is the go-to poster man for grief. He lost his sons, property, and wealth and battled his health. Everything in his life was a challenge—physically, mentally, emotionally, spiritually, relationally, financially, etc. He was in a constant nightmare that wouldn't let up. His suffering was great, but his faith was remarkable. He barely held it all together, but he never stopped focusing on God. I think that's the key.

When I was in my early twenties, the man that I thought God wanted me to marry walked away. I was devastated and heartbroken. I uprooted my life, changed colleges, and moved cities. In the middle of that pain, I couldn't see it was the best thing for both of us at that time. All I could feel was heartbreak. Then two months later, I was in a bad car accident. My car was totaled, and I was in constant physical pain. Doctors fed me pills, sent me to physical therapy, and said that it was all in my head. It felt like my world was caving in all around me. Suddenly, I'm grieving the end of that relationship *and* the damage to my physical body. I had to change how I did everything because of this one accident.

I would love to say I had steadfast, unwavering faith like Job, but I didn't. My grief turned into years of confusion, mistakes, and questioning God. Even with shaken faith, I still prayed. They were small and perhaps empty prayers, but I still clung to God even though it was only half-hearted. At that time, I didn't have the emotional intelligence or tools to help me when I was struggling.

I was so numb that I had to force myself to watch sad movies so that I would cry. Have you ever done that? My go-to films to get the waterworks flowing were *Steel Magnolias* and *The Notebook*. I would let the tears fall for a couple of hours and use a whole box of tissues, and then I would feel better temporarily. Though my grief was messy and tricky, I remained hopeful.

Speaking of hope, let's turn our attention to the New Testament. Matthew, Mark, and Luke in the Bible include a story of a woman hemorrhaging blood for twelve years. Can you imagine?! If you have a uterus, you know how desperate you might feel if you were in her position. But this woman was willing to take drastic measures to get a breakthrough. She heard the news that Jesus was coming and mustered up some strength to go out and army crawl on her hands and knees in a crowd full of people. She reached for his robe, and because of her faith, she was healed.

Perhaps this is a familiar story, but let's look at it through the lens of grief. Imagine, for a moment, this woman's life. She saw doctors without any answers to her questions. She tried anything and everything to get beyond her constant discomfort and pain. On top of that, she was embarrassed, tormented, and isolated from everyone. She didn't have a life. She didn't have a family to support her or friends to lean on. She was an outcast because her physical body was sick. Talk about an emotional roller coaster!

This woman isn't a typical example of grief, but can you see it? She had a deep internal struggle between her body, mind, and soul. Her body was waging war on her, but even after twelve years, she never gave up hope.

Being willing to turn to God for our physical or other needs is an essential step in this process. God's waiting for us to have that if-I-can-reach-his-robe-I-will-be-healed kind of faith. What would happen if we got more desperate like this unnamed woman?

Whatever you are facing right now, your entire being is feeling it. The degree of impact is different for each person. Some might experience a lack of appetite, headaches, or insomnia during grief, and others might land in the hospital.

The goal is to become aware of grief's impact on our daily lives and understand that it impacts our internal and external world. It's easy to give up hope when you feel like your life is falling apart. You start questioning your life. You think about quitting God or maybe even life. Instead of pulling away from God, I'm encouraging you to lean in, even though it's complicated.

We see a few common threads through the life of Job and our unnamed heroine. We all go through things that bring us to our knees. We all experience grief, which can manifest itself in many areas of our lives. The key is shifting our focus and reliance from "self" to God. This shift happens when we keep our focus on the One who breathed life into us. Then, we have an opportunity to fall on our knees, extend our arms, and invite Him into our pain. We need to see God as our partner in grief instead of the One who caused these awful things to happen. We live in a fallen world. The losses will keep happening. So how do we arm ourselves with the tools we need to deal with it? What happens when the season you're in lasts two years, twelve years, or even fifty years? What will you do then? Will you remain cold, bitter, resentful, and hopeless, or will you fight for yourself? Will you do the work and ask the tough questions that push your buttons and prod your soul so you can find some spiritual relief?

CHAPTER 5

The Driver's Seat

When we experience a loss, we think we have everything under control. The truth is we can't move forward until we get to the point where we are willing to let God take the reins. We have to embrace the pain and let someone help.

Do you remember Hagar? She was the Egyptian servant of Sarai and Abram. Hagar is in a tangled web of lies and soap opera-level drama. In Genesis 16, Sarai is taking matters into her own hands. She longed and prayed for a child, which wasn't happening according to her timetable. The solution was to make Hagar the surrogate to get her family started.

After Abram and Hagar were intimate, jealousy waged war in their household. The angry looks, bitterness, and resentment were happening around the clock. Trust did not exist. Hagar was disrespectful to her boss, and Sarai paid her back with a mean kind of vengeance. It got so bad that Hagar ran away.

An angel met Hagar and told her to go back to Sarai because she was pregnant with a son, who would be named Ishmael. To have to go back to that hostile environment was a giant pill she had to swallow. But she was committed to following the Lord, so she did.

But as you might imagine, this was not the ideal living arrangement. It was a chaotic situation. Ultimately, the newly named Sarah and Abraham had a son, Isaac. Tensions ran at an all-time high, with the adults having issues and kids in the middle. Finally, in Genesis 21, Sarah could no longer take it and made Abraham do her dirty work and dismiss Hagar and Ishmael.

Hagar left her home with her young son. Can you imagine the level of grief she was experiencing? She lost her home, job, the father of her son, friends, and the everyday familiar life. It was all gone.

Abraham, Sarah, and Hagar chose to take control of the situation. As a result, there were many unintended and unforeseen consequences. Even though their choices brought deep sorrow, God still honored the parents and poured his goodness on both children, Isaac and Ishmael.

From Hagar's point of view, she was over it. She was overwhelmed and upset by all the chaos. The situation she found herself in became unmanageable. When Hagar ran away and had her encounter with the angel, she had a choice to make. She could keep running or go back and deal with the fallout. Ultimately, Hagar wanted God's promise fulfilled for her son and descendants. To do that, she had to make a decision, changing her heart from "I give up" to that of humility and willingness to stick it out.

Sometimes we are brought to our breaking point. We aren't sure if we can go on. We wonder if God is even there. Does

He care? But God will meet us where we are, no matter our thoughts and feelings, if we posture our hearts and let Him.

The bottom line: Abraham, Sarah, and Hagar didn't trust God. They didn't think God would follow through with his promises. They were aging and didn't think a child would be possible, so they crafted an I-know-better-than-God plan. This solution created a storm of intense emotions where deep-seated fears boiled to the surface.

When we come up with our own solutions, it usually doesn't go as planned. What would happen if we partnered with God and turned it over to Him? It can be challenging. Grief is complicated. It's an internal tug-of-war. But we need to get to a place where we are willing to let God take the wheel. Why?

The heaviness of grief is a burden we were never meant to carry on our own.

We've discussed our emotions and thoughts when grief hits us like a crashing wave. We've examined how we "cope" and "handle" grief. But how can we make small and practical changes that will make a difference in our day? Grief is a process, and we are all in different places. Sometimes we can't get out of bed; other days, we may need something tangible to get us from sunrise to sunset without feeling like we are losing our minds. Perhaps the grief is overwhelming, and you're angry at God and everyone. Maybe you are further along with your grief but still burst into tears at random times. Perhaps you are ready to open up to your friends and share your struggles. Wherever you are, let's look at what we must do to prepare our hearts for the practical.

Point of View

When things are happy and going well, how do you view God? What about when things are so complicated that you want to bang your head against the wall? Do you see Him differently?

Growing up with the hellfire-and-brimstone preaching, my view of God was that He was sitting on his throne, judging every little thing by writing all the good stuff down. More importantly, He was putting all of the bad in capital letters. It felt like God was criticizing, correcting, and teaching me through tough love and hard life lessons. These clichés circled in my head: "Everything happens for a reason," and "God doesn't give you more than you can handle." So I thought He caused those bad things to happen because I needed to learn something. With this line of thinking, I unknowingly judged myself and others more harshly. And while God is the ultimate judge, it's not His heart toward us.

He's the Creator of life. He is a Father. He loves us. He wants to spend time with us. He wants the best for us. So when we go through tough times and put Him in the box of judge, jury, and executioner, it creates a wall that divides us. We think God allowed or even caused these things to happen in our lives. That can make you more guarded and closed off in your relationship with Him, which can spill over into your relationships with others.

God is a gentle God. If we hear Him whispering corrections to us that are harsh and negative, that's the enemy speaking. God corrects us in a gentle, loving, and kind way. He is love, joy, peace, patience, kindness, goodness, faithfulness, and self-control. If it doesn't fall within these lines, then it's probably the enemy. God will not call His creation stupid, fat, ugly, dumb, selfish, or horrible.

When going through seasons of grief, I had to switch my view of God. God is there to love us and bring peace that passes all understanding. God wants to bring us true comfort and rest that can only come from above. God has the grace for every emotion you have, even if you are yelling and questioning His motives. God has heard it all, and He is not surprised by our anger or frustration. God wants an invitation into our grief.

Repair and Redefine

We might feel broken inside when grieving, as if pieces of our heart, mind, or soul are missing. It's crucial that God first repairs our inner chaos. Grief must always be mended. The messiness we have on the inside needs a higher power. No amount of food, sleep, exercise, shopping, dating, drugs, alcohol, busyness, or whatever your coping mechanism is will be able to sustain you. I learned that the hard way.

When we are willing to invite God in, He breathes His gentleness and grace on us to repair our heartache and pain. Once He does that inner surgery on our hearts, He can take it and redefine that experience for us, renewing our minds. It doesn't mean God helps us "forget" or "get over" our grief. Instead, He takes the broken pieces and mends our hearts.

Sometimes we resist this step (I'm looking at myself here). We have already tried it, and nothing has changed. I've said the same thing more times than I can count. But this isn't something to check off your to-do list. It's about an *ongoing* conversation and relationship. Think of your best relationship. How often do you stay in contact? The best relationships are typically the ones where you stay in constant communication. How's God any different? If you still need a breakthrough, pray again. Ask again. Believe again. Remember, it's a process. All you have to do is take one step forward. Then another.

Sidebar: It may seem like you are dealing with your grief and feeling more at peace. There will come a day when you feel proud because you are progressing and have taken five steps forward, but something will happen, or you'll have something trigger you that will recall the grief back to your mind. In those moments, it will feel like you got knocked backward ten steps. The secret is to expect this to happen. That's life. Don't get disappointed when it happens. Instead, try to have a "just in case" plan where you call a friend, get up, and take the next best step forward all over again.

Intense Emotions and Fears

Have you ever felt that your grief is heavy and overwhelming? It can be downright intense. In desperate moments, you're down on your knees. Tears and snot are streaming down your face. You're asking, pleading, and yelling at God. *Where are you? Are you even listening to me? Do you even still care? Have you forgotten me?*

Grieving can make you feel like a deer in headlights—you don't know what to do or how to feel. It's all you can do to put one foot before the other and try to live "normally."

The book of Psalms is a constant go-to. It's real and raw. It's full of the entire rainbow of human emotions ranging from the darkest dark to the lightest light. David is expressing his most genuine feelings. We are peeking into his "Dear Diary" moments and seeing the ins and outs of his real walk with God.

David gives me hope. After all, David was blessed, despite his worst human moments. That says God can still do something beautiful with all the ashes we've accrued. David allowed God to do inner surgery, but it was a lifelong process of communicating and being willing to give it all to Him.

It boils down to this: What has to happen for you to trust God with your pain? Do you have to get to a point where you hit a new rock bottom?

Let me be clear. Allowing God to be in the driver's seat is not about turning your back on your loss. It's not getting "over" the person you loved or who passed away. But at some point, your emotions and feelings cannot continue running the show. At some point, you have to say, "This is hard. I cannot do this alone. I need a higher power to help."

Don't punish yourself by wandering your wilderness, circling the same terrain repeatedly. If insanity is doing the same thing over and over and expecting a different result, then the Israelites were out of their ever-loving minds. It's easy to judge them. They were so close to their promised land!

We do the same thing. We relive our nightmares. Sometimes we make progress, but it never feels like it's enough. We don't feel a sense of relief. We take five steps forward, only to be shoved ten steps back. But that's life! It's a process.

And this process boils down to questioning our faith. When we experience death and tragedy, it's natural for us to ask questions. Most of us, at some point, will have a crisis of faith.

You'll wonder, *What do I believe and why? Because that's how I grew up? Have I adopted my faith from my family?* These are normal questions.

Discussing the doubts that come with chaos is essential when going through life's losses. But sometimes, it seems like it's a taboo subject. We're afraid to be judged, so we skip these honest discussions that lurk in the secret corners of our minds.

It's easy not to talk about it because you wonder what others might think. It can take time to walk through it; however, let me encourage you to let go of any guilt and shame that may be lingering. Questioning one's faith in times of hardship is entirely normal.

Take a look at some of these scenarios. Have you ever asked God when:

- You lost a job and wondered when you'd get your next paycheck?
- Your loved one died?
- Your health took a turn for the worse?
- A life was taken from this world too soon because of a tragic accident or suicide?
- You've been praying for the same thing for decades?
- You lost a child?
- Someone betrayed or took advantage of you?
- Your friendship goes sideways?
- You didn't know how to get beyond your depression?
- You're struggling with an addiction?
- A marriage comes to an end?

These and other tragedies can easily lead us down a path where we doubt and question our faith. Think of it this way, when you have a glitch on your computer, sometimes it locks up and freezes. The little cursor wheel is spinning, and it's not completing your desired action because it is stuck. So, when all else fails, you hit the power button and shut it down. Once it reboots, it usually fixes the issue. So, what you need is a restart.

What caused your spinning wheel to stall your conversations between you and God?

It's a fight to power through these questions, but posing questions makes way for conversation and reflection. You can't get to know someone better through statement-making dialogue. You have to ask questions, get curious, and be open to what awaits you on the other side.

When ready and willing, here's a prayer to position your heart. Pray this until you believe. Change it up. Use your words, but let it sink deep into your spirit.

"Father God, I am ready and willing to give you this next phase of my journey. I want to turn my grief over to you. These emotions and thoughts are taking over, and I admit I'm not coping well. I invite you into my situation right here, right now. I want you to be in the driver's seat and take complete control. I realize that I've tried to handle everything on my own. I've tried to be strong for everyone around me, and the weight of this burden is too much. I place it in your hands and say, Let thy will be done. In Jesus's name, Amen."

CHAPTER 6

The Art of Surrendering

How do we surrender our grief to God when holding on to someone or something we've lost?

When we resist, the enemy has a field day. The enemy doesn't want us to surrender our grief to God. If we try to do that, the enemy whispers these lies:

- "You will fall apart."
- "You will never recover."
- "God has better things to do."
- "Just ignore it; you can handle it on your own."
- "Others are depending on you to stay strong."

In these moments, we need tools to escape that mental minefield.

Work was my go-to emotional outlet. At first, I overworked and avoided emotions and feelings from a relationship that ended, but then it snowballed and became a habit. I didn't even realize it. I was being ambitious, career-driven, and focused on my goals. Changing cities, jobs, and climbing the ladder was good, but it gave me a false sense of control.

But something started to change. Phone calls and text messages saying that my co-worker has breast cancer. Another has brain cancer. Another has pancreatic cancer. Another has a rare lung disease. When you start hearing this news, it gets to you. Then you start getting phone calls saying these beautiful and talented souls passed away so young, in their forties and fifties. It makes you stop and think.

You take a step back and start to evaluate your life. We were all working long hours in the same fast-paced industry. Your question is, who will be next? You wonder about your choices and how you got to where you are in life. Who is this person in the mirror? And that, my friends, can kick off another aspect of grief.

Ultimately, something was missing in my life. I'm a Bible believer. I'm meditating, praying, and reading my devotions. But I wasn't going to church regularly. After I experienced what I thought was a heart attack with massive chest pains, I decided that I needed a break from my marketing career. Although I was grateful for my job, I needed a break from that world. That led me to pursue other passions, but there was a problem. I brought all my workaholic tendencies into that too.

A business coach of mine introduced me to a counselor by the name of Linda. We started doing the Workaholics Anonymous program. It's similar to Alcoholics Anonymous (AA) or Narcotics Anonymous (NA), but for people who work too much. It sounds ridiculous, but it's truly a real thing.

At first, I didn't want to do it. I didn't think I had a problem. But God usually brings people into your life for a reason, so I thought I would go with the flow. I went through the twelve-step recovery process of Workaholics Anonymous, which helped me see patterns in my behavior.

This program is one process that led me to surrender. You hear all about surrender in Sunday school or preached from the pulpit at church. We sing songs about it. Arrogantly, I thought I knew what surrender was all about. But there is a vast difference between knowing and experiencing. I had to finally experience it to truly understand.

Surrendering is not a one-time thing. It's a daily recommitment.

Life is an emotional roller coaster that takes you on twists and topsy-turvy turns. Then it's a sharp right turn that jerks your whole body around, almost giving you whiplash. It happens to us every single day. In this life, it is a guarantee that you will experience grief, loss, and pain. But there is another guarantee. You don't have to do it alone.

Jesus is the perfect example of surrender. He struggled with grief in the Garden of Gethsemane, located at the bottom of the Mount of Olives in Jerusalem.

He took Peter, James, and John with him. Did He need these three men to come with him? No. He could have gone away by himself, but He didn't. He had a support system nearby.

In Matthew 26:38–39, "He told them, 'My soul is crushed with grief to the point of death. Stay here and keep watch with me.' He went on a little farther and bowed with his face to the ground, praying, 'My Father! If it is possible, let this cup of suffering be taken away from me. Yet I want your will to be done, not mine.'"

When praying to His Father, Jesus positioned himself with humility and reverence. He got on his hands and knees with His face pressed toward the ground. He knew what was coming, but the weight of it was overwhelming.

Jesus's life is a model for us. Jesus was a spiritual being on His human journey. During His time on Earth, He had people He confided in. He wanted to be free of His suffering. He was battling His emotions, but He was willing to yield what He wanted to His Heavenly Father. But He had to do so multiple times. That's why surrender is not a one-time thing. It may need to be an hourly or daily recommitment, especially during grief, heartache, and pain.

In Luke 22:43–45, "Then an angel from heaven appeared and strengthened him. He prayed more fervently, and he was in such agony of spirit that his sweat fell to the ground like great drops of blood. At last, he stood up again and returned to the disciples, only to find them asleep, exhausted from grief."

The disciples were exhausted from being in this dark and gloomy atmosphere. It was too much. They couldn't even stay awake.

Meanwhile, Jesus continued to pray. The level of stress that He experienced was unthinkable. In these moments, He showed us the importance of having a support system. He showed us that we need transparency with our emotions, and that there is always a need to talk to our Heavenly Father. He modeled how we have to position our hearts to be willing to turn it all over to God for His ultimate purpose. Jesus surrendered it all.

We will never do life perfectly. But we can take some of these lessons and translate them into the world we live in today.

The good news is that we've already done some prep work in the previous chapters. So you're already on your way to living from a place of surrender.

First, you've been exploring your pain, getting curious, and asking yourself questions. Second, you're finding acceptance where you are and permitting yourself to feel. Third, you're using the tools in your toolbox, such as journaling, calling a friend, or talking with a professional coach or counselor. Whatever it takes to get your grief out.

It's all about exploring your emotions, feelings, and thoughts but not getting stuck in that place. You want to access and acknowledge your feelings, but you don't want to become them. Grief is not your identity.

You've been sifting through your life to see who is in the driver's seat. Discovering where you go first, God or Google? You've identified the coping mechanisms that keep you stuck in the same rinse-and-repeat cycles. Nothing is changing. You might feel better temporarily, but it doesn't last. You know these patterns are not sustainable, so you must relinquish control and become a willing vessel—a willingness to turn things over to your higher power. You must detach from what you think your life should be.

Detaching is hard when you have a particular view of how your life "should" be. It's not supposed to be this way. That loss was not supposed to happen. It can be hard to adapt when a change occurs, like a rug pulled from underneath us. Who are we relying on? Who are we trusting? We must find a spiritual and inner knowing that God is bigger than our grief.

Now that you've gotten a head start, there are three other important points to understand when surrendering your grief to God:

1. Dig deeper and get to the root.

Our beliefs determine the lens through which we view the world. Beliefs are grounded in our emotions, thoughts, childhood, and life experiences. That's why we must dig deeper and go beyond what we think and feel. We must get to the root of what's happening because it can subconsciously create a false belief. False beliefs impact how we navigate our lives. Let's walk through an example. If you are feeling sad, ask these questions and journal your responses:

- Why are you sad?
- What caused the sadness?
- Did something trigger you?
- Where do you feel sadness in your body?
- How have you observed other people handle their sadness?
- What do you believe about it now, and how does that impact your life?

If I was going through this exercise, here's an example of my answers:

- I'm sad because I miss my grandparents.
- The cause is that my grandparents have both passed away.
- I was triggered because everyone was talking about the holidays. This Christmas was the first year I didn't get to celebrate with them.

- When I'm sad, it can create tension in my head, neck, and shoulders.
- I've seen other people handle their sadness in silence. They deal with it privately in their own time.
- Based on these answers, my beliefs are: when you experience sadness, you should keep it to yourself and deal with it alone. We need to set our feelings aside so that they do not impact our day-to-day responsibilities.

As you can see, this can unlock what you believe. Go through this exercise for every emotion or thought that is a struggle—anger, fear, shame, guilt, pride, resentment, sadness, or whatever else you are struggling with. Ask God to reveal what you believe about this situation. Is it a God-based belief or a false belief? Be willing to look at it and say, "What can I learn from it? What is this trying to teach me?"

Kids grow up with a natural tendency for curiosity. Their favorite question is: Why? As adults, we still ask this question. We want to know the logic and reason behind something. Why did this happen? Why did they act that way? Why don't I feel better? Answers may elude us, but it creates an opportunity.

God is calling us to go deeper in our spiritual walk. We must remove the weeds that have taken over and replace them with higher truths. Find those verses that speak to you. When in doubt, start in the Psalms. Remember, grief and loss is a process of self-exploration that takes time.

2. Commit to constant communication.

You may need to surrender your grief to God more than once, or you'll quickly feel like nothing has changed. This whole concept was frustrating to me at first. First, I would get annoyed and snippy with God. Then, after journaling and praying, I would question why everything still bothered me. I followed all the steps but thought I wasn't doing something right.

That's when I realized two things. First, I had to start each morning by surrendering to God. Secondly, there needed to be constant communication throughout the day.

Life happens. You need a simple way to reconnect with God when your day gets off track. It sounds overwhelming, but it doesn't need to be. Instead, you can whisper, "I surrender this day to you, God. Let Your will be done. In Jesus's name, Amen." Over time, I realized that this process was unraveling the pain and allowing me to see it from a new perspective.

3. Create habits and rituals to stay accountable.

Do you like structure or hate it? My personality likes it, but I need freedom too. I can quickly become bored. I had to find different ways to recenter and authentically connect with God. Although it took me a few years, I created a morning and evening ritual. In the morning, I say a prayer that has three different parts.

First, I use a version of the Modeh Ani. A Jewish prayer of gratitude is said when rising out of bed in the morning. The original version is:

"I offer thanks to You, living and eternal King, for You have mercifully restored my soul within me; Your faithfulness is great."

Next, I combine it with Lamentations 3:22–23, "The steadfast love of the Lord never ceases; his mercies never come to an end; they are new every morning; great is your faithfulness."

Finally, I end the prayer with a call to surrender as Jesus did in Matthew 26:39. When I put it all together, the prayer goes something like this:

"Blessed are you, Oh Lord, King of the universe. Thank you for returning my soul with compassion. Abundant is your faithfulness and love that are new every morning. I surrender my day, plans, desires, and schedule to you and say, Let thy will be done. In Jesus's name, Amen."

Every morning we wake up, it's new. We get a reset. It's important to acknowledge the giver of life and feel grateful that we have another day to make a difference.

Another favorite is a Native American prayer I came across from Nick Polizzi's The Sacred Science website:

"Dear Great Spirit (or God), You are inside of me, within my very breath, within each bird, each mighty mountain. Your sweet touch reaches everything, and I am well protected. Thank you for this beautiful day before me. May joy, love, peace, and compassion be part of my life and all those around me on this day. I am healing, and I am healed."

Now at the end of the day, before bed, I do a nightly candle ritual. Life can be chaotic. We are constantly on the go, with our minds racing a mile a minute, so this forces me to pump the brakes and slow down. This ritual is a simple breathing practice. Here are the steps:

1. In the evening, before bed, light a candle, and turn off all the lights.
2. Pick a comfortable spot to get quiet and still.
3. Take a deep breath in and out.
4. Focus on the flicker of the flame.
5. Start listing all the things you are grateful for and the blessings you experienced throughout the day.
6. Pray for people who pop up in your mind.
7. Talk to God about what you are feeling and thinking.
8. End the prayer by surrendering everything that happened in your day.

It's all about repetition and finding ways to stay connected with God. If you learn how to surrender to God daily, it will strengthen your spiritual muscles. In addition, it will bring a sense of clarity and meaning in times of grief.

But fair warning, going through this process is uncomfortable. It will push and stretch you to your limits. So here are some things to expect on your journey:

- You will never fully understand why things happen the way they do.
- There are invisible forces that want us to stay stuck in our pain. Remember, we are spiritual beings on a human journey, so there are a lot of things that we don't see. These forces will do their best to keep you in despair, which means you will face resistance. You might be doing great one day, and the next, you might feel like you will lose it in the middle of the grocery store. That's okay. It happens to all of us.

- Your circumstances seemingly aren't changing, which could mean a few things. 1) You need more time. Maybe you've been numb for so long that you need more time to tap into what you think and feel. 2) You need to fine-tune this process and tailor it more to your life. Take the concepts and figure out habits that will support your life. 3) It could mean you are trying to do it all alone. It may be time to get additional support through a coach or counselor.

When we go through difficult times, we want things to change instantly. I believe God can do miracles; however, I think more often God makes subtle changes in and through us over time. In these moments, He is teaching, healing, and strengthening us from the inside out. Be encouraged and look for those subtle shifts over massive miracles.

CHAPTER 7

Releasing the Unresolved

Do you have any regrets or feel like things are unfinished? Grief can often linger when unresolved issues remain. That can leave us stuck. We must take time to go beyond the surface and explore this side of grief. Underneath it may lie feelings, regrets, painful memories, or things left unsaid.

This is all easier said than done. In my experience, there is an unspoken Christian "good girl" code of conduct. We need to keep everything together—no outbursts, and we can't let anyone see us behave in a manner that may be questionable or "worldly." It's this constant pressure that leads many to behind-closed-doors addiction. The need to be perfect and never sin is crushing. But here's the newsflash: we live in a fallen world that is not our forever home. That means we all mess up. Instead of admitting to it, we cover it up. No wonder there is such a distrust in the church and with religion. As topics such as mental health are more widely discussed, we do begin a steady progression toward the future.

How does this apply to grief? As we've touched on previously, we know that it's possible to experience every emotion under the sun when grieving a loss and the last thing you want to do is admit it out loud.

So instead, we say nothing. We pretend everything is fine. But we are slowly dying with each fake smile that crosses our faces. Shame and guilt have us in a constant cycle of self-abuse. I'm all too familiar with regret, and with the act of second-guessing yourself after the fact. Here's what happened to me.

Father's Day was my grandfather's last day out of bed before he passed away. We were giving medication every four hours around the clock. He couldn't move on his own. He wasn't eating. We couldn't turn up his oxygen—it was on the max ten-liter setting. He looked like he was in constant pain. But he couldn't communicate well and tell us what was happening. That's when my mind started to spin.

Are we doing enough? Perhaps we should try this or that?
How do we make him more comfortable?

I wasn't sleeping. I was in pain from all the lifting, pulling, and manual work that goes into caregiving. Tensions were on the rise. It was exhausting, and I was in need of a break.

Intuitively, I knew he had only a few days left, and it would only get harder—on him and on us. If I went back home, he would pass away while I was gone. I needed a break, though. I found myself at a crossroads and didn't know what to do. I decided that if a ticket was available on the flight I wanted, I would book it and go home. If it wasn't available, then I would stay. I rationalized it, saying that if God wanted me to stay, I wouldn't be able to get the plane ticket.

But I did, and I left. And three days later, on July 4th, I got the call that he had passed away. It was only supposed to be for a few days, but I had a cold, and had to take a COVID test. I didn't count on waiting a week for the result, which meant that I missed my grandfather's funeral.

Guilt flooded me, and I jumped on that what-if hamster wheel. From the outside looking in, it seemed selfish to leave. I was wondering if I made the right call myself. But I had to follow my instincts based on what was happening. And there was a lot of good that came from it. Conversations happened that were much needed. Others were able to step in and help. But that didn't stop the anger, frustration, guilt, and shame from piling up.

Let's dive in and uncover how to handle these uncomfortable topics, so that we can be free of this inner turmoil and continue the healing process. But, before going into how to release these natural and all-too-human attitudes, let's touch on something that can get overlooked.

Perception vs. Reality

What happens if people loved the person who died, but behind closed doors, they were a completely different person? They could have been sweet and kind to everyone else and hellacious in private. Or they seemed unapproachable in person, but they were dependable, loyal, and the glue that held everything together behind closed doors.

Perception can be tricky when it comes to the grieving process, especially when others really didn't know the person the way you did. Unresolved feelings can arise when there is a disconnect between how the public perceives your loved one and your personal experience.

Ruminating about what a person did or how they treated you can leave you tied up like a pretzel. If you can't process your emotions or feelings and begin to unravel those knots, it can impact your life and health for years to come. If this sounds like you, consider reflecting and doing the exercise at the end of this chapter.

Past Losses

When we experience a loss, we often (whether we realize it or not) recall past experiences with grief. For example, have you ever noticed that when a loved one passes, you think about all the other people in your life who have passed away?

This is often referred to as cumulative grief. Another example of cumulative grief is when you experience a loss, and before you can wrap your head around it, there is a second loss. An example would be your loved one passing away, then your pet, and next, a friendship or relationship ending. In these multiple-loss moments, we may feel overloaded with deep grief. There are many layers to peel back, and that's why this is a process.

Negative Emotions Taking You Over

Sometimes emotions like anger, guilt, and shame come up on the pathway to grief. It can feel like you are on a hamster wheel of emotions, wondering when the mad scientist overseeing your experiment will have mercy and let you go free.

Anger is a common emotion; however, it's also a smoke screen that is a camouflage for something else. That means we must focus on these feelings to let go of them.

You're angry. What about? Have you felt this way before? Why do you think you were triggered? What's the root of the anger? Are you upset because this person you loved left you all alone? Are you mad because of a traumatic experience with this individual? Anger is a typical response that falls under the umbrella of grief. But it's dangerous to stay stuck in it.

These types of emotions can become toxic if we avoid or ignore them, potentially leading to self-destructive behavior and talk. If left unchecked, anger can turn into rage. Guilt and shame can imprison us—keep us locked in a dark hole of solitary confinement, focusing solely on our failures and mistakes. To get beyond the anger, you need to deal with it so that these emotions don't fester.

These "bad" emotions can guide how we can grow as human beings. We can learn from all of life if we are open. If we do, we can choose a different way to react or respond when difficult situations arise. That means you could improve the outcome of your current circumstance because you learned from the past, gaining wisdom from the past and not allowing it to rule your future.

Have you ever said, "Life isn't fair"? We all have at some point. My friend said: "Life isn't fair. Fare is what you give the bus." And she's right. You may not get justice in this world. You may not get the answers you want or have your life turn out how you wanted. It may feel like God is nowhere to be found and that He has stopped fighting for you. But He hasn't. Our point of view on Earth is from our eyes only. It's not the big picture.

And the bottom line is that it's out of your hands. We have absolutely zero control.

But you're on the path to doing the deep, inner work. To be frank, what you're going through sucks. But I want to congratulate you on being brave. You are working toward being open, honest, and willing to hand your heartache to God. Even if you aren't quite there yet, you're trying—and that counts for something.

To release these negative emotions, feelings, and thoughts, we need to look at ways to reduce these feelings. The next step is to evaluate if there is any unforgiveness lurking around in the shadows.

Forgiving Who?

Did you know that whether we choose to forgive, or not to forgive, impacts us physically, mentally, emotionally, and spiritually? With grief, we hold things in. If we want to eliminate the heavy weight on our shoulders, we must do some deep inner work. You may want to take a second look, even if you have nothing or no one to forgive.

Believe me, I get it. I used to think that I had nothing to forgive, either. But when I started diving deeper into my grief, I uncovered that I still held on to the should-have-done or should-have-said moments that replayed in my mind. I realized that I still felt guilty for being a tough manager, losing my patience as a caregiver, losing parts of myself in relationships, and being unable to be there in person for my grandfather's funeral. These things can eat away at us and infiltrate how we act, think, and respond to life.

Most people carry around with them some form of unforgiveness, whether from childhood or life's losses, that keeps piling up. From Martin Luther King, Jr., to Mother Teresa to Jesus, they have all talked about the power of forgiveness. It's written in sacred texts and taught by political and social leaders; however, it's still something we need to focus on more than we do. If we all (me included) reach for compassion, empathy, and forgiveness to understand others, perhaps this world would be a better place. So let's look at how these change-makers thought of and valued the concept of forgiveness.

Interesting fact, forgiveness is in the Lord's prayer. In Matthew 6:9–13:

"This, then, is how you should pray: 'Our Father in heaven, hallowed be your name, your kingdom come, you will be done, on earth as it is in heaven. Give us today our daily bread. And forgive us our debts, as we also have forgiven our debtors. And lead us not into temptation but deliver us from the evil one. For if you forgive other people when they sin against you, your heavenly Father will also forgive you. But if you do not forgive others their sins, your Father will not forgive your sins.'"

But what if that person keeps hurting you over and over again? Keep forgiving them because several chapters later, it states in Matthew 18:21–22:

"Then Peter came up and said to him, 'Lord, how often will my brother sins against me, and I forgive him? As many as seven times?' Jesus said to him, 'I do not say to you seven times, but seventy-seven times.'"

Did you roll your eyes? I had that reaction in the past when someone used scripture in this way too. But it illustrates the point. If the concept makes you angry, then it's something worth exploring. God knows your situation, and if it was important enough to include it in the Bible, maybe we need to give it a little more attention because many of us are harboring and withholding forgiveness whether we realize it or not.

Often, we confuse forgiveness with accepting how a person treated us. Forgiveness is not condoning their actions. Forgiveness is extending grace and understanding that we all have moments where we say or do things that hurt others. Forgiveness recognizes that no one is perfect and ultimately prioritizes peace.

Ultimately, the truth is that forgiveness impacts you, not them. It sets *you* free.

Sidebar: True forgiveness isn't about criticizing the person each time they do wrong and reminding them every time they've screwed up. Recalling the past and bringing it up in an argument to make your point is not true forgiveness. And if your loved one has passed away, we still find ways to bring it up. For example:

- "Well, when your father was alive, he never did that."
- "We always did it this way."
- "You don't love me like they did."

If you find yourself upset and starting a statement that recalls past conversations like the above, it's time to pump the brakes and tune in to what's happening inside of you.

Forgiveness is a complicated process, but doing the inner work on your journey is worth it. Don't take my word for it; here are a few quotes from some famous people who made an impact around the world:

Mother Teresa said:

"People are often unreasonable and self-centered. Forgive them anyway. If you're kind, people may accuse you of ulterior motives. Be kind anyway."

Reading this one might sting. Gandhi said:

"The weak can never forgive. Forgiveness is the attribute of the strong."

Gandhi was right; it takes a strong person of character to forgive. But, to extend the thought here, we are all human, so it's okay if this process takes time. Grief, life, and love is all a journey, and it's not about being perfect.

Martin Luther King, Jr., put it more eloquently when he said:

"Forgiveness is not an occasional act; it is a constant attitude."

Forgiveness is an olive branch we extend to others. We can let go of that hurt so it doesn't negatively impact us. These may not be parts of grief we widely talk about with our family or friends, but it's a natural (and normal) aspect of loss. So if you have any unforgiveness hiding in the back of your internal closet, consider this exercise. It will be like spring cleaning for your heart, soul, and spirit.

Resolving the Unresolved Exercise

Grief may feel different for you. You grieve, but you didn't really know the person that well, or maybe you never loved them. Or the relationship was complicated. Or you have mixed emotions, or in some cases, you feel nothing. You are numb to it all and have no feelings. Even though this individual is no longer here, you can still communicate what you wanted to say but never did.

Let's put all this into action. This is for you if you have:

- Unresolved issues from loved ones who are no longer living.
- Anger toward the deceased.
- Feelings of guilt or shame that have you second-guessing yourself.
- You think about all the should-have-said or should-have-done moments.
- Negative scenes replaying in your mind.
- Days filled with the ups and downs of grief's emotional roller coaster.
- Any unforgiveness hiding in your heart toward others or yourself.

This exercise came from a former coach, Camden Hoch, and I have also completed similar processes with other coaches. This format has been slightly adapted for those dealing with grief. This ritual will release these unresolved emotions, feelings, and thoughts.

Step 1: Set aside at least thirty minutes.

Step 2: Find a quiet place where you won't be disturbed. Lock yourself in a closet or bathroom, or car if you must.

Step 3: Pull out a piece of paper and a pen. Yep, we are kicking it old school on purpose.

Step 4: Use the questions and prompts below to help your thoughts flow.

Sit and get comfy as you step into a quiet environment with your paper and pen. Take three deep breaths to center yourself. You can even put your hand over your heart, allowing for a deeper connection and getting in touch with your innermost thoughts.

When you're ready, here are some questions to help prompt your pen:

- What's unresolved in your life?
- What do you wish you could have said or done but never got the chance?
- What happened that made you second-guess your decision?
- Why are you angry?
- Why do you feel guilt or shame? If so, explain.
- What do you regret most?
- Do you need to forgive a loved one?
- Do you need to practice self-forgiveness?

On your piece of paper, list anything and everything that comes to mind. It could be one instance or one hundred. No filter. It can be related to your recent loss, or it can be things from your past. If it seems unrelated, write it down and try to take your time with the process. Figure out why the thought came to you.

You won't be sharing this with others, so this isn't the time to hold back or censor yourself. Now is the time to get all of those hidden emotions and thoughts out of your heart and head onto paper. Find freedom in the action.

Pro tip: Light a candle and gaze at the soft, glowing light. This can deepen your connection and aid your time of reflection.

Step 5: Select one of your unresolved moments from your list. Start with the one that keeps circling around in your mind the most or keeps you up at night.

Step 6: Next, write down everything that happened in full detail. Include things that were said and your feelings about what occurred. No fact is too small. This is the time to get it all out.

Step 7: After you finish this exercise, walk away for a couple of hours or return to it the next day. When you come back to this letter, write down anything else you may have forgotten.

Step 8: Once you feel like you have written everything about that situation, you'll want to add this paragraph at the end.

"I, (insert your name), release this into God's hands. I surrender it all to the One who created the universe. Today, (insert date), I lay it all down at your feet and ask that you remove these emotions, thoughts, and feelings from my mind, body, and soul. May you fill my heart with peace and help me to see your light and goodness in my life. Let thy will be done, in Jesus's name, Amen."

Step 9: Once everything has been written down, read the prayer above out loud.

Step 10: The final step is to take a match and safely burn the letter to release it. If you don't want to mess with fire or don't know if you can safely burn the paper, then tear it up into little pieces and put it into the trash.

Important: Do not put this in the recycle bin. We don't want to recycle the letter or its content; we want it gone.

Note: You may need to do this exercise multiple times for the same situation. Often, when we go through traumatic losses, we uncover different feelings as time passes. Plus, if you brainstormed more than one situation, you may need to do this exercise several times for each.

Feel free to adapt this ritual to your beliefs and make it your own. Some people might call this closure, but it's the beginning. It's another point on your journey. When we get unstuck from the unresolved, it helps prepare our hearts to open up to others.

CHAPTER 8

Trusting Others
With Your Tears

How can we trust others with our deepest hurts and tears? Let's face it; trust does not come easy. In fact, it's more challenging than ever considering the state of the world around us. Being cynical and skeptical is common practice. Being guarded is second nature.

Who can we confide in? Where do we find people who will get it? In this chapter, we will uncover why we need to open ourselves up to others and how we can do so in a practical way that makes us feel seen and heard. Instead of shying away and isolating ourselves from people, we must find the trusted few with whom to share our innermost thoughts, feelings, and tears.

Have you ever been through a significant change but didn't want to share it? Of course, you want to, in theory. Perhaps you even realize how it might be helpful, but something stops you.

People try to relate to your grief, but you know that they don't fully understand. So when they give examples of their grief, you find yourself dismissing it, and deciding that it is a lesser grief than your own.

People mean well, but sometimes it feels like they are trying to "fix" you, as if you can fix grief. Sometimes you don't need advice or solutions. Instead, you need someone to listen and love you in the brokenness because that is where you are right now.

Have you or someone you know ever pushed someone away after a loss? Have you been the one pushed away? They may be in shock from a loss and don't know how to deal with it. Their world has been turned upside down, after all. What was once familiar is now foreign. This sudden change often leads us to push people away and isolate ourselves rather than lean into support. We feel less like a burden that way. If we handle it on our own, that would make it easier for everyone. Or would it?

I'm an introvert. I can be extroverted in specific settings, but my natural go-to is hanging back and observing. I'm very opinionated and don't have any problems speaking up for myself. However, as I've gotten older, I realize I don't always need to share that opinion with others, so I choose my moments more carefully. Because work has always been a part of my identity, I want to come across as a knowledgeable professional. While that is good in some settings, sometimes it makes me unapproachable. When I left my career, I became more aware of this go-to behavior after I took a break from my marketing career. So, being open and vulnerable takes extra effort.

But it's essential to learn how to trust others. What would it look like to be more open and vulnerable? What if we viewed vulnerability as a strength, not a weakness?

It can give us a greater internal capacity for compassion and kindness. It can allow us to grow from all of life's experiences. Finally, it also allows us to pass on what we've learned to others and lead us to our purpose. For these things to flow naturally in our lives, we must reflect on the possible roadblocks that may be in the way.

A few deterrents stop us from moving into a place where we can be open to discussing our grief in all of its gory detail. It goes beyond the "I'm doing fine," "Hanging in there," "Getting better each day," or "It's rough, but I'm good," responses. That's surface-level conversation. I'm talking about diving into the nitty-gritty feelings that we often hide because we are too embarrassed or ashamed that we are having these thoughts. And if you've been grieving for a long time, you may find that you feel as though you can't bring this up to those around you because you "should be beyond it by now."

As we've stated before, grief is a personal journey, so reflect and consider where you are now. Then, think about what personality traits you want to see in a person you hope to confide in. What do you need at the moment? What kind of characteristics in a person would make you comfortable sharing your story? While this is not an exhaustive list, here are a few things that typically hold us back from feeling safe.

Confronting the Cycle of Distrust (The Past)

In previous chapters, we've discussed the importance of getting curious about our emotions and innermost thoughts. In addition, we've discussed the importance of reflecting on our past to see trends in our present moments that help shape how we respond in the future. If we don't take the time to reflect, it will feel like the same things keep happening to us.

What often gets in our way when it comes to sharing our grief is how confidants have abused our trust in the past. Maybe they took your story and gossiped about you. Perhaps they judged and ditched you as a friend. Perhaps you found the courage to share; however, they reacted in a way that made you shut down. So now, we justify not talking to anyone because we don't want to be a burden. It's easier to shy away from it than to lean into it.

In those moments, we feel like we overshared. That can leave us embarrassed and feeling as if our story isn't worthy of someone caring and listening.

What it boils down to is people from our past hurting us. And now, we have more difficulty trusting and opening ourselves up to others. We fear the same thing will happen again. As if that wasn't enough to keep us silent, we may have close friends with whom we'd love to share our story, but with one hitch. If we speak it out loud, it makes it more real. We don't dare utter the words out loud because that would release the chains we placed on ourselves. Thus, we end up saying nothing and suffering in silence. We secretly hope that if we swallow it down and keep it locked inside, our pain will eventually disappear. But instead, we are living in a state of shackles and chains of our design (rhinestones optional).

Unspoken Expectations

Another deterrent that piggybacks off the last point is that we may have certain expectations for those moments when we *do* share our hearts. So there is this disconnect between what you hope happens and what really happens.

Perhaps you want to find a person who has been through *exactly* what you have experienced, but your search turns up empty. You don't know whom to trust with these thoughts because no one will understand what you're thinking or feeling.

Perhaps you feel that once you share your burdens, the weight will fall off your shoulders and finally solve the ache within your soul. But clearly, the grief is still there.

We may even find that people want to swoop in to save you or figure out how to "solve the problem." You're unsure how it happened, but sharing your pain somehow turned into a brainstorming session that you never wanted. This type of experience makes you want to lock your stories in a vault tighter than Fort Knox, never to be heard of again.

Proving Your Pain

Speaking about the chaos circling in the corners of our inner world takes bravery and courage. But, unfortunately, when we do have the courage to share, sometimes we feel like it's a slap in the face because someone chose to belittle what we are going through to prove that their pain is greater than ours.

Have you ever started to share something personal only to have someone say something like, "That's nothing compared to my situation," and then they go on telling you why their life is worse? This response is another deterrent from opening up to others.

Some play this who-has-it-worse role effortlessly and consistently with everyone they meet. But, then, some aren't trying to put your pain down. Instead, they tried to relate but needed to communicate more clearly. How do you tell the difference between these two types of people?

Depending on your relationship, you can talk about how their words made you feel and what you're experiencing when they take over the conversation. It may be innocent, and belittling you was not their intention.

Have the conversation first; most of us make assumptions and snap judgments about what others do or say. We often fill in the blanks with our beliefs and what we think that person meant by that comment; however, often, we are wrong. So, it's important to calmly ask for clarification and discuss before deciding how to proceed, especially if this wasn't the first time they've offended you and you've been considering ending the friendship. It's complicated to sort through all of this when grieving, so make sure you have boundaries, and if you don't feel comfortable sharing with that person, that's okay too.

Have you ever wondered when grief became a contest? I know it's a strange question. But when I was thinking about this chapter, it came to me repeatedly as if it's a game to see who has the worst story.

My story is worse than your story, so there. It's like people are still on that kindergarten playground—na-na-na-boo-boo. That should never be the goal. One-upping each other's stories can have soul-crushing side effects. It's one major hurdle that we must jump over to allow ourselves the gift of sharing. And it goes both ways!

Even if you both had the same type of loss occur, every person's experience is unique. That means you may be able to relate to the grief, but the details surrounding the story are different. We have different backgrounds and paths that lead us to where we are, and that's a good thing. That's not something to look down upon or dismiss. When we feel these gnarly emotions bubbling to the surface, let's show each other grace. Our experiences and stories are how we relate to each other. We have an opportunity to hear with our hearts the pain someone is going through. We can learn from each person's experiences in this life—if we are open to it.

Vulnerability

The next roadblock on our path is how we view vulnerability itself. We touched on this a little above. I used to think that vulnerability was a weakness. You open up and trust that the other person has true intentions, only to find that they don't. However, sometimes those life lessons can come at a steep cost and impact us physically, mentally, emotionally, and spiritually. It makes sense that our approach to vulnerability may be altered after things happen.

Being vulnerable can make us feel exposed. That's why we want to feel a sense of safety. If there are any hints of possible betrayal when we start chatting, our mind is trying to discern if we can relax and open up or if it is time to get out of there.

As if that weren't enough to wrap our minds around, being vulnerable can be emotionally draining. You feel like your entire being is on edge because you expose parts of yourself like open wounds. After all, you don't share with just anyone!

It's not that we need to share every little detail about ourselves or even the situation we may face. It's an authentic expression of where we are now and what we are experiencing in life. There is no doubt that grief puts us in a vulnerable state.

That said, vulnerability is a superpower, albeit a scary one at times. But if you're willing to risk telling the story deep within your heart to a trusted friend, it could make a massive difference in both of your lives. So you're sitting, crying, sharing—what a world this would be if we would make the time to be there for each other.

Now that we've discussed potential deterrents or roadblocks, we can begin cultivating friendships and creating a sacred environment that allows us to share our struggles safely.

Consider Private Contemplation

Before you embark on sharing, take time for self-reflection. After experiencing a loss, it can be difficult to trust other people with your grief. So take the time to acknowledge and understand your feelings first. Sometimes we must wade through the fog and mud to process our experience. Clarity will take time; it comes piece by piece, not all at once.

Choose the Right Person/People

Write a list of people who you would feel comfortable sharing your story with. Carefully consider your criteria before making your selection. What qualities and values do you want in this individual? Can you trust them not to gossip after your chat? Look for people who share similar interests, experiences, and beliefs as you, which will naturally provide a basis for mutual understanding.

You may only want to share with one person depending on your personality and situation. Or, if you're more extroverted, you may want to share with multiple people. One caveat, I recommend you select someone who does not live with you. You can share with those under the same roof; however, I would pick an additional person not involved in your day-to-day routines. It allows you more freedom to express all feelings surrounding your grief in greater detail.

If, for some reason, no one springs to mind, that's okay. A coach or counselor may be best, as confidentiality is the foundation of their practice.

Connect

Once you have reflected, pick your person and choose a supportive friend(s) who will listen without judgment and offer emotional support. Next, reach out to them and explain what you want to do. This step is informal. But it's helpful to let the other person know you want to chat about what you've been going through in your grief journey. You don't want to ambush them. Grief and loss are heavy topics. You may even mention that you put a lot of thought into it and chose them because of the mutual respect and trust in your relationship.

Create a Plan

After you connect with the person, set up a time when you're both free of distractions. Plus, when talking about grief, our emotions may be all over the place. So you need to select a space that allows you the freedom to get things out. That could be at someone's house or a public park. If you feel comfortable going to a coffee shop, that's cool. But think through it. Would you want to be seen crying with mascara-stained cheeks and people interrupting you to make sure you're okay? That could be annoying and limit your openness, so plan accordingly.

Communicate What You Need

You've probably noticed that grief changes daily and from moment to moment. So on the day you decide to meet, you may have different emotions that you weren't expecting that are all of a sudden coming to the surface. That's okay—honor where you are in the moment. But do respect the plan and each other's time. Don't be afraid to tell your friends how you feel about something or share the details about what's going on in your life—both good and bad—so that there is an open line of communication between both parties involved. Most importantly, communicate what you need at that moment. Are you seeking advice? Do you need to vent and let everything out? Do you want a shoulder to cry on? Do you want to brainstorm solutions? Do you need to include some irreverent humor and laughter? Let them know! It's vital to address this up front.

Because many of us jump into problem-solving mode when someone is talking to us about a problem, we must be clear about what we need when we decide to share. Don't forget to be flexible and go with the flow of the conversation.

Ultimately, this process is about creating a safe and sacred space that allows you to share without fear of judgment. Think of it like a sanctuary. Tapping into our tears and trusting others with what's in our hearts can be scary and overwhelming. We never know what people will say or how they will react. Here's an example:

Christians can be overly concerned with perception, especially from other believers.

- "I'm not a good enough Christian if I drink this glass of wine."
- "If I say that word, then somebody will judge me."
- "If I talk to my non-Christian friend, what will people say?"

As if they will take away our get-into-heaven card! So we pretend and wear our masks. But then, when we do get the courage to open up, it's such a watered-down version. It may be the truth, but it's not the whole truth. We end up downplaying our human moments to where they aren't relatable. Ultimately, we are here to love each other and learn from our experiences in life. How can we do that if we don't feel comfortable sharing?

When worrying about what others might think, sharing our innermost thoughts on grief and loss can be tricky. It's incredible how much our conversations are ladened with niceties and pleasantries but offer no substance. Dare to be an emotional, vulnerable hot mess with those you trust. Perception is a part of life whether we like it or not. That's why taking time to reflect and cultivate relationships where you know you feel seen, heard, and supported is vital to our lives. Remember, you are not alone; we're all a work in progress.

CHAPTER 9

Power in the Pause

What happens when we feel like our journey with grief comes to a standstill?

Chances are you've gone through difficult seasons before in your life. Perhaps your previous losses are not of the same magnitude as today's, but you've still grieved. And if life has taught us anything, it is that things happen—good, bad, and everything in between!

But what do you do when you've hit a wall in your walk with grief? You feel like you've been doing all the "right" things but still have trouble. Let me set your mind at ease, first. What you feel is normal. It just might be time to roll your sleeves up and create a plan to get to the other side of your current battle.

When disaster strikes, some people have an emergency go-bag. We had to do that recently when a wildfire started in our area due to a fallen power line during super dry and windy conditions. Thankfully, we didn't have to evacuate. The experience taught me how I was incredibly unprepared if I had to leave at a moment's notice. When I was packing my go-bag, my mind filled with questions. *What do I bring? How is this happening right now?* I felt overwhelmed and lost, walking in circles to see what I needed to grab.

When it comes to grief, the unexpected will happen regardless. I'm not talking about having a step-by-step plan with every detail outlined. But if you are grieving and having a hard time with all the overwhelming emotions and thoughts circling you like sharks in chummy water, then it's vital to have some tools you can reach for when the pain becomes too much. Let's look at a few roadblocks that might come up in your journey.

Expectation 1: You will get hit with a tidal wave of grief repeatedly and randomly.

When I was caregiving for my grandfather, there were a few times where I was by myself so that my mom could get a break. Because my grandfather would need assistance, I ran any errands for the day before he got up in the morning. One day, I finished getting the groceries and got into the truck. Out of nowhere, I burst into tears in the grocery store parking lot. I had no idea where the waterworks came from because I wasn't feeling sad or PMSing, but clearly, I needed to let out some of the emotions that I had been stuffing down. Most of my grief usually hit me when I ran errands, in the shower, or crawled into bed. Of course, your experience with grief will be different from mine. But you can expect random things to trigger your emotions and tears at various times.

Expectation 2: Life won't go back to the way it was before your loss.

During the grieving process, it's a guarantee that you will be on an emotional roller coaster. However it happened, your life is changing, and it will never return to how it once was. You may struggle with a setback or two, even when you think things have settled down. You've gotten into a new rhythm and a "new normal." Then all of a sudden, you're on the roller-coaster ride again, being jerked around so fast you get whiplash. You find yourself dazed and confused because, in one moment, you were seemingly okay, and the next, you feel like you're upside down, unsure as to what end is up.

The world we once knew is gone. We feel discouraged and empty because we desperately want to go back. We find ourselves stuck in a loop of "if only's." If only we had more time. If only I could say what I never dared to speak before. If only we could share one more moment. We dream about it, wake up, and then the harsh reality sets in. Life will never go back to how things were—it will only move forward to a different type of normal (whatever that is).

Expectation 3: You'll get tired of being strong.

Grief can be a constant daily battle where you are fighting to keep your head above water. There is so much you have to do. It's like you are fighting to survive, and it's a struggle to keep putting one foot in front of the other. But you still have things to do and endless responsibilities. So we put on our superhero masks and keep marching or flying forward. But you can only do so much before the weight on your shoulders tips the scales, making you face-plant in the dirt.

"Fake it till you make it" will only get you so far. It won't help long term when you are suppressing your feelings. That dam will eventually break. You will be exhausted, tired, and maybe feeling a little (or a lot) on edge. It gets to the point where you don't want to be "the strong one" anymore. You want someone else to carry the crap because you don't know how long you can keep going this way.

If you are a self-reliant introvert, like me, you internalize a lot. You deal with a lot on your own, things that nobody else knows about. I used to think I could do everything on my own. I could handle anything that came my way. The simple truth is this: no person can get through life solely on their own. I've had to learn to open up, share what I'm going through, and be vulnerable. It doesn't come naturally to me. True strength is reaching out in moments of weakness. Otherwise, it's just called survival.

Expectation 4: Well-meaning opinions from others will drag you down.

Different people may come out of the woodwork telling you what you need to be doing and how you should spend your time. Most people mean well. They aren't trying to upset you on purpose. People want to help and be supportive but don't always know how. It's not a subject taught in school. And depending on the type of grief you are experiencing, you may hear all sorts of opinions.

You know the saying about opinions, right? They are like buttholes. Everyone has them, and they usually stink. So sorry for that slightly irreverent joke, but it does make my point.

Joking aside, when we talk about grief, people typically mean well when giving unsolicited advice. And if something they say connects with you, great; if not, try not to hold it against them. Extend a little grace and remember they may not know what to do or say. Plus, they aren't in your head. They don't know what you are thinking or feeling. They aren't mind readers. Hearing all the platitudes may be exhausting, but you may have to let things roll off you like water on a duck's back. Should you have to do this? Nope. But it's a reality of the process.

Expectation 5: You will never understand why.

Many times we want to know the "why" behind something. Confusion, doubts, and questions flood your mind:

- You don't know why God allowed this to happen.
- You don't understand why bad things happen to good people.
- You don't understand why someone you loved was ripped away too soon.

In this life, we won't get all the answers to our "why" questions. Even if we did, we still wouldn't understand it. It's hard to wrap our minds around the fact that much of our lives are out of our control. We can manage what we do, how we respond, and what we say. But we cannot control other people or what happens around us, leaving us on shaky, unfamiliar ground.

Any loss can make you cold and distant. You are pulling away, retreating, and numbing out. It can leave you hopeless, as if God and others have betrayed you. Self-destructive habits become part of your daily routine, but nothing fills that empty void in your heart. A true sense of surrender is getting to a point where you know that you will never have all the answers to this life's painful twists and turns and finding a way to be okay with that harsh reality.

It can be incredibly overwhelming and discouraging when we are at a grief standstill. You may feel that you are no closer to finding answers or healing your heartache than when you started this journey. You start wondering if you shoulda-coulda-woulda done something differently. It's normal to feel alone, confused, and frustrated—but know that you don't have to stay stuck.

There is never one solution to any problem. However, what I've found is that the solution doesn't always have to be complicated:

- We need to understand that how you are grieving (even if you feel like your progress has come to a complete stop) is natural. Find solace that everything you are experiencing is part of the process.
- We need to learn to recognize patterns, which will give us clues on how to navigate our grief.
- The key is to explore what tools will work best for you and where you are today. God often brings us clarity in unexpected moments and through unforeseen sources.

So, what do we do when the stuff of life hits the fan?

If you feel pinned up against the wall, it's time to resurrender. Acknowledge where you are at today, think about what has you feeling stuck, accept that this is where your journey is for the moment (be honest and admit how you feel), and be willing to say, "I am not in control and powerless over this situation, and I need help from God."

This framework may sound familiar because we discussed it earlier in the book. However, surrendering is not a one-time thing. When I find that I am fighting against the troubles surrounding me, it means I am trying to handle everything in my power.

Many people talk about casting away their cares and giving all their hardships to God. But it's not a one-time deal. Our human nature wants to say, "I'm good now; I got this now, God." We try to take back control, so a constant tug-of-war is going on. We turn over our troubles to God and take them back until we can't handle them anymore. Then we give it back to God, and it's a continuous game of hot potato.

Surrendering is similar to meditation in that it is a practice. However, to get the full benefits, we need to be consistent with it.

I used to think I couldn't meditate because those voices that ran through my to-do list told me all about how I could be spending my time getting things done instead of sitting here. They would get *so* loud every time I attempted meditation.

But once I learned that this is normal and everyone experiences it, it made meditation easier. Finding stillness and shutting off the chatter in my brain was (and still is) challenging. Even now, my mind races with thoughts of things I need to do, errands to run, and everything else that is worrying me on any given day. I have to push through the voices to find the stillness.

As a recovering workaholic, staying busy was my coping mechanism. But I had to get to where I was *willing* to shut up, get quiet, and be still. Of course, it's all easier said than done; however, it's worth it.

Here are a few tricks that helped set the stage to make meditation easier:

- Light a candle and stare at the flame. This technique allows me to bring my focus to the present moment by simply staring at the flickering light.
- Journal first to get the to-do's out of my head.

- Take a hot bath or shower.
- Play instrumental music. My favorite is Native American flute music or tunes you would hear at a spa or yoga class.
- Add essential oils or burn incense to calm and relax my mood.

Does the idea of stillness scare you? Sometimes we avoid hitting the pause button. If we sit in silence, then we start hearing things.

The voices in your mind get louder, reminding you of your to-do lists, errands to run, people you need to call, or even negative self-talk. On top of that, your mind is chattering away, and you want to throw in the towel. The whole process can make you feel on edge. How can I connect to God this way? Who knew being still would be such work? But it does take effort on our part.

It's easy to feel like you are losing your mind when you have moments of intense grief. Do we want to "feel better" now? Many use busyness as a way to distract themselves from the emotions and feelings they carry around with them every day. Although it seems counterintuitive, when we quiet our minds and get still, we extend an invitation that gives God room to work.

There will be a time when distractions are needed. Then there will be times when you need to vent, and others when you need to shut up and reflect. And there will be times when silence and stillness are your best friends.

When you are at a standstill with your grief, you may need to do the opposite of what you are doing to shift gears. For example, you may need to get quiet and be still if you are constantly busy. On the other hand, if you have been reflecting a lot, you may need to shake things up and get active.

No matter your activity level, have a heart attitude or "heart-itude" that hands over the reins to God, especially if you are struggling emotionally. ("Heart-itude," see what I did there? I love a good word mash-up.)

Explore and find the tools that resonate with where you are right now. You might be surprised by what you learn through this experience. Find encouragement in the simple truth that pausing life's busyness and being still can bring us to another level of healing.

CHAPTER 10

The Sands of Time

G rief is not a linear process. It's not as simple as one, two, three. It's not a formula or mathematical equation you can solve. Grief is messy and complicated, and it doesn't ever follow the path we expect it to in our lives.

Many grievers think they "should be over it by now," but they still grieve. Depending on the expert or source, grief can last from six months to two years. After that, grief may crop up here and there, but theoretically, it should no longer consume you. I know that through my personal experiences, coaching, and listening to the stories of those who have come across my path, everyone is different. We each differ in our approach to grief and how we choose to handle it, which can vary from loss to loss. That means the length of time that grief may last is different too.

Time is a fickle thing. It happens whether we want it to or not. We want more time with our loved ones. We want less time doing chores. We want to fast-forward through our lives when we are kids. We want to slow it down as we get older.

When a loved one dies, we think about our time together, wishing it were longer. We believe that we need to be "over our grief" and not show it after a specific amount of time. Sympathizers are around at first, even to the point of being a hindrance. But then the well-wishers stop checking in as the weeks and months pass. You may have wanted that at the time, but now you hear crickets, and it scares you. It's a bizarre and mysterious feeling—that the world keeps going when your world falls apart. This chapter covers how time impacts our journeys, from intruding thoughts to calendar events that trigger us to conversations that fade, questions we raise, and how grief can seemingly stretch for eternity.

How do you react when you hear these phrases?

- "God won't give you more than you can handle."
- "Time heals all wounds."
- "This too shall pass."
- "It's part of a greater plan."

Did you notice any physical reactions while reading those common sayings? I bet most of them were negative. Perhaps you rolled your eyes, crossed your arms, tightened your jaw, your shoulders became tense and rose to your ears, etc.

We hear, and maybe even say, some of these common phrases throughout life. And while there lies some truth, they can be very irritating when you are going through an emotionally turbulent time.

In my opinion, time does *not* always heal all wounds. What it does is give you distance from it.

When your loved one leaves this life and goes on to the next, people are there at first. But it does end. As more time passes, fewer people check in. And you're still left with this loss.

Everyone else's lives keep going, and meanwhile, you feel:

- A war is waging internally each day.
- It's a constant struggle to keep it together.
- Weak and helpless, not strong.
- Like there's no hope.
- Beyond lost.
- It's the worst pain you've ever experienced.
- There is a giant hole in your chest.
- Like the other half of you is missing.
- Incomplete and broken.
- There is no light at the end of the tunnel.
- Life is unfair.
- Like questioning why they are gone and you're still here.
- Angry at God.
- Like you believe, but your faith comes and goes.

So, you feel like you are drifting alone in the sea with no anchor. The emptiness surrounds you as you drift farther and farther away from the shore. You're lost and left with a big hole in your heart that seemingly will never be filled. But time keeps marching on, and we do our best to paddle our boats.

We may do well for a while. You take five steps forward, and then the calendar strikes. You get triggered because of a birthday, anniversary, or song, which makes you feel like you got shoved ten steps back. It's like you are swimming in the deep end of your grief all over again, which makes you feel like you are drowning and about to go under.

Time keeps ticking whether we want it to or not. As we walk through grief, we think about the past, present, and future. We think about our mortality and all the should-have, would-have, and could-have been moments. If only we could turn back the hands of time!

Some people will tell you not to live in the past while grieving. Don't focus on what you lost when that person died. Don't focus on the marriage that just unraveled. Don't focus on that job you didn't get. When these losses happen, we can easily start taking inventory of all the losses we've ever historically experienced, which can compound the effects of our feelings and thoughts.

Then you get other advice that says to focus on being in the present. Focus only on the good before you, not the past or the future. Living in the present and being mindful are trendy grab-our-attention words that give way to all sorts of tips and tricks to help us stay focused on what's in front of us.

And then we are warned about looking too far ahead in the future! But setting goals and determining what we want our life to look like down the road is an important exercise too! You can make plans and have a vision, but typically a lot of unexpected stuff comes up. Twists and turns that you didn't see coming and you can't plan for in life.

When we are going through the grieving process, time will be a trigger for us in many ways. The past, present, and future are essential to reflect on together. You can't separate one from the others because that can leave you stuck in the past, neglecting the present, and daydreaming about the future. So it's essential to look at time as a whole and how it can impact us.

Additionally, we often think about our mortality when we think about grief. When we're younger, we feel invincible. We live not thinking about consequences or appreciating what's in front of us. Sometimes ignorance truly is bliss! Whether we are young or old, there comes a point when more deaths occur, disease is rampant, and suicides are commonplace. It's happening left and right. One person passes away; then you hear news of another, and then another. It's a domino effect. The more you lose, the more aware of loss you become.

In these moments, when we are dealing with life's losses, we start wrestling with our mortality. We think about the number of people we lost. We think about how this family member died at eighty and how we are nearing that number. We think about how this family member got diagnosed with a particular disease, and we can start calculating our likelihood of getting it too. Perhaps the older we get, the more we face mortality when illness and tragedy strike.

Nothing is wrong with this thinking if it doesn't lead you down a never-ending rabbit hole of fear. But, remember, life is a teacher, and each experience is a lesson. So, asking ourselves questions, seeing patterns, and having a healthy sense of wonder can be good. It can allow us to step back and assess our lives to bring about positive change.

When someone you love dies, it's natural to think about time. The time you lost or wasted. The time you didn't take a chance. The stupid fights. The words you wish you had said. These thoughts are a springboard for reflection, not a place you want to stay stuck or live in permanently.

From a clinical perspective, grief can be tricky, especially as it relates to time. Experts say you typically experience your most intense grief from the moments right after it happened up to eighteen months after your loss.

Is that true for you? Only you can answer that question. But if you picked up this book, you are trying to figure out how to process it all. The fact that you are tired of pretending and willing to face your grief is brave. So give yourself credit.

If you grieve quickly, then some may think you haven't spent enough time dealing with the loss. On the other hand, if you grieve too slowly, some may think you are not moving through the process fast enough. There are many technical terms and types of grief, but regardless of the labels, we all go through various experiences and process things differently.

So, does grief have an expiration date? It seems to have a social and public expiration date. But privately, that's another story. And it doesn't matter if you are an introvert or extrovert; much grieving happens behind closed doors.

Is it possible for one's grief to be reawakened? Absolutely! The calendar is often the trigger. Important dates like anniversaries, birthdays, holidays, or the day they went to heaven. A "heaven-versary," as my friend Nikki likes to call it.

But in some cases, it can feel like the intensity of grief never lifts. This type of grief has many clinical names, such as complicated, deep, or prolonged grief. It can seem as if the tiniest thing triggers us, and we feel like we are reliving the trauma and loss all over again. It hits you like a tidal wave, knocking you flat on your butt.

Sometimes those hits keep coming. It can seem as if life is giving you nothing but a series of back-to-back hits to the face. The financial bills are stacking up, your kid is acting out, your pet dies, and a close friend was diagnosed with cancer. Those hard knocks keep coming one after the other in a when-it-rains-it-pours kind of way.

These moments fall under the category of stacked grief, where we are grieving all of those hard knocks in life, from the big to the small. Whether we realize it or not, we carry that around with us. That leaves you emotionally, mentally, physically, and spiritually overwhelmed. You are barely hanging on. You are suffocating and finding it hard to breathe from the emotional heaviness of everything around you.

It's not uncommon for crappy things to happen one right after the other. It's a common phenomenon. If you are experiencing the same or greater intensity as when your loss initially occurred, you may want to seek professional treatment. Feelings of intense grief typically come and go with time. But if it's constant and those flashbacks, nightmares, and haunting thoughts can feel like they have a hold on you and won't let go, you may want to consider getting help to process what you are going through. It's admirable to try handling it on your own, but it's even more courageous when you acknowledge that you need help.

"Complicated grief" is a medical condition that many people have experienced. It may seem odd that I'm focusing on this a bit, but we have got to take off our masks. Grief is normal, and it's time we acknowledge all aspects of grief. Finding hope again is more than possible; however, you have a part to play. It won't come to you from nowhere. You need to ask soul-searching questions and take that first step that seems almost impossible. You can do it, and you are not alone.

We'll observe and see things from different angles as we dive into those soul-searching questions. For example, time is our most valued asset. But when we talk about grief, it can be our greatest enemy. So the doubts and questions are nonstop:

- *How long will I be grieving?*
- *Can you start grieving before your loved one dies?*
- *When will I stop feeling this way?*
- *Why am I still here and they are not?*
- *Why do I feel so broken?*
- *How can I go on when a piece of me is missing?*

The hustle and bustle of our day-to-day life has time passing faster than we realize. Our watches become dictators. Yet the sand flowing through the hourglass is always running out. What happens when a loved one is seemingly healthy and then six months later is gone? It doesn't make sense. It's unfair and leaves us questioning.

Time means something different to each person. It can be your friend, and it can be a ticking bomb. We all know that we can use our time wisely or waste it. Productivity can seem like an uphill battle when you are grieving. You may feel constantly distracted, and your lack of focus might be at an all-time high. It's normal. I promise you, it is.

Dealing with losing a loved one is a heartbreaking and distressing experience. It's a time when sorrow, numbness, guilt, and anger can overwhelm us. But with self-reflection and time, we can process these feelings, and the intensity will slowly fade.

Throughout this process, our mindset is something we need to keep tabs on. You may have moments of dark, depressing, and melancholy moods, or you will have moments of laughter. You will find moments of comfort and peace, often in the small things.

We think there is no time to cope because we must be strong for others and all life's other responsibilities. So then we beat ourselves up because we feel we should be over the grief by now. But, then, as if that weren't enough, there are numerous questions circling our minds:

- *How long will I feel this way?*
- *Will I ever be happy again?*
- *Why are they gone and I'm still here?*
- *Will I always be alone?*
- *How will I make it through this?*

So we wear our masks and pretend we got it all together. After all, we don't want to be known as a "Negative Nancy"! So, keeping quiet is the smart choice. That way, we don't bring others down by the pain we feel on the inside. And more questions bubble to the surface:

- *How can we be true to ourselves and where we are now in our journey?*
- *How can we be honest with others without coming across as a negative person?*
- *Do people want you to be honest about how you feel?*
- *How can I connect with others when struggling to get through the day?*

Honesty is not being negative. But we are *always* judged by what we say. At least, that's how it feels. Perception is a very real thing. There is a social stigma about how to grieve, and it's one that changes depending on where you are and who you are talking with.

For instance, at work, you might get a couple of bereavement days and are then expected to return as if nothing happened and perform your job the same way, even though your whole world has changed. On the other hand, you may be lucky and have a boss you could open up to and who is empathetic toward your situation, giving you flexibility and leeway in your work. And then again, maybe you have someone who doesn't care and thinks you should get over it and not talk about it in the workplace. You might have a job that doesn't even offer a bereavement period!

Various unspoken social "rules" will dictate how you present yourself in public. When you get home, you get to strip down and remove all that social politeness and let it out. But sometimes, this can look like you are taking your frustrations out on your loved ones. This behavior often shows up when we are struggling and, at the same time, stuffing down our emotions.

Let's take a moment to highlight that we need to keep an eye on our internal temperature gauges:

- What are we thinking and feeling?
- Are we aware of what's happening inside of us?
- Are we taking on too much?
- Do we need to have better boundaries?
- Do we need to open up and talk with someone?
- Are we leaning on God or dealing with it in our strength?

When we are in a deep state of emotional pain, soul-searching is a much needed thing. Grief is a multi-level life disruptor. So we must pay attention to what's happening in our body, mind, soul, and spirit.

So, how can we turn these questions into something positive? It's in those tiny millisecond moments where we find gratitude or appreciation.

When I talk about gratitude and grief, it usually is met with some eye-rolling, folded arms, and a heavy amount of cynicism. I totally get it and relate. Because I have been there too—some days, I am still there. But what I want is for us to find *moments* of gratitude. I didn't say to be in a permanent state of fake happiness or toxic positivity. For example, these are some questions to think through:

- How can we remember all of the good memories from the past?
- How can we find gratitude for what we have today?
- How can we see the blessings in our tomorrows?

From birth, parents joyously mark their child's milestones. When kids are in school, time goes by so slowly that we desperately ache and long for the days when we're out in the world as adults. When we're adults, we blink, and the year is over. We wish to be kids again. And when we get on up there in years, days can creep along as it gets physically taxing to move around. No matter what part of life we are in, it's easy for us to become captive to our watches in one way or another. We can get stuck in the past, ignore the present, and question the future.

You may be in the thick of grief right now. It's not that you will "get over it," but as time passes, the intensity lessens. You'll think about your grief and loved ones differently. That doesn't mean you think about them less or forget about them entirely. But it shifts, from the intensity of loss to their impact on your life.

As time passes by, you get distance from your original grief. And each step taken can offer a different perspective. Looking up close, you will see all the nitty-gritty details, casting a seemingly enormous shadow over you. But if you look at an object from far away, you can see the shape, but the details are fuzzy, and the shadow becomes smaller and smaller. So everything depends on your point of view and where you are at that moment. While it may not seem like it now, your perspective will shift over time.

We want to get to a point where we have more perspective. We start to have moments of gratitude. And you see that there is a time for everything and that wherever you are today is normal. So it's okay to stop pretending, but understand that time isn't against you. Time is a teacher.

The good news is that God doesn't operate in time. He meets us where we are and provides the grace we need in each moment as long and as often as we need it. There is no getting over it. There is no getting through it. The encouragement is in this: allow this experience to be part of you because that person that passed from this life to the next is part of your story. Setbacks will happen. Yet in the middle of the unknown, take comfort that your paths crossed, and they made an impression on your life.

When my grandmother passed away in 2016, it was tough. I remember not crying at the funeral. I couldn't let myself go fully into that point of all-consuming grief. I was afraid that I might not be able to stop. Being one of her live-in caretakers, the last few months had been rough. I had cried in the shower countless times because I knew what was coming, especially when she went from palliative to hospice care at home. So for me, grief started early. We stayed to help my grandfather for almost a month after she passed away. When we left, I wrote on a yellow Post-it note: "One minute, one hour, one day at a time."

So I pass these words on to you.

CHAPTER 11

An Open or Closed Valve

The physical anatomy of our hearts includes four valves. When the valves are open, they allow the blood to flow through our bodies. When the valves are blocked or closed, it can cause severe health issues and even death.

We need to view ourselves like a heart. It's easy when we experience grief to close ourselves off. We hide from the world. We put on a mask filled with fake smiles and social pleasantries. We are holding it together, and we can manage. But is that the way God envisions you to live life? We can keep closing ourselves off to others or open our hearts again and get beyond the barely-hanging-on survival mode we've been living in for weeks, months, or even years.

Have you ever gotten bad news, and the moment you heard the information, you couldn't believe it was happening? For example, you may have gotten word about a sick relative while you were living in another state, or found out that someone you love was in a car accident. Your mind hears the information but simultaneously pushes it away. At least, that's what happens to me. It's my way of protecting myself.

Our amazing bodies have an innate radar. So when a perceived threat happens, we typically choose one or more of these responses: fight, flight, flee, or fawn.

The fight means I'm about to take my earrings off and throw them down to protect myself and others around me.

Flight is I'm not dealing with this mess; peace out. I am running like there are hot coals under my feet. Insert movie reference, "Run, Forrest, run."

Freezing means that I'm not moving a muscle. When you see a cat, and they notice you looking at them, they freeze because if they hold still and don't move, perhaps you can't see them.

Fawn is a more active yet passive approach. Let's see how pleasant I can be, and if I can calm the situation so that it doesn't become a world war.

But the threat doesn't always have to be real. Our brains are so powerful that sometimes when our minds recall a memory and bring it to the surface, we relive it all over again. When I get bad news, sometimes I shut down and pretend that I magically disconnected a wire from my brain to my heart. I get all stoic, and for a while, I trick myself into thinking that I'm not feeling all the emotions that this lousy news bubbles up to the surface. So I try to distract myself and stop myself from thinking about the problem because I don't want to break down and cry.

While this can be a short-term way to "cope" when receiving unpleasant information, it's not a long-term solution. If done in excess, it can lead to being closed off.

Your mind will do all it can to protect you against feeling your feelings. This self-preserving tactic happens because it's afraid to go to that place and lose control.

In these moments, it's natural for us to push people away. After all, talking with people, even our closest friends, about what we are going through can sometimes seem like agony. Putting words to your pain can seem as overwhelming as the loss itself. You are in a constant state of emotional overload, and you are barely keeping your head above water as it is. It becomes easy to slip into silent mode. Perhaps you don't mean to isolate yourself; it's naturally happening. Or you are doing it purposefully because you think it will be better for everyone involved. Either way, it's all a means of self-protection.

There is no right or wrong here. Sometimes you don't want to talk about life because it's just too much. Then there will be a time when you are ready to vent it all out. For those moments in between, consider finding a positive outlet, such as a physical activity that helps you get it out. I loved kickboxing because I felt I could vent my frustrations on the boxing bag in front of me. If you sense yourself keeping it all in, find something that could work for you. It could be knitting, yoga, running, gardening, kickboxing, puzzles, painting, writing. Anything that holds the mind's attention and offers a bit of relief. Just remember to be gentle and kind to your body.

When you're ready to open up to people, here are a few tips to help you ease into the process.

If you are going through a hard time, you may have to think about it in terms of those you live with and those you don't. If you are emotionally struggling, those living with you will pick up on your subtle *and* not-so-subtle cues. You may be able to hide your feelings 95 percent of the time, but those who see you on a daily basis will notice what's oozing out of those emotionally busted seams.

It's essential to be up front with those living with you and let them know you are struggling but doing your best. Let them know that you are processing your grief, and they may notice you being on edge sometimes. You don't need to force yourself to share when you aren't ready, but at least acknowledge where you are in the process with those around you. It's necessary for their sanity and yours.

Select one or two people to open up with at first. Choose people who do not live with you. For example, you can choose a relative who may be experiencing the same thing as you or a friend who is willing to be there and listen. In these moments, it's important to revisit what we talked about in Chapter 8, Trusting Others With Your Tears.

It's all about setting boundaries. Setting boundaries with those around you adds a layer of self-protection so you don't overextend yourself emotionally. You don't want to force yourself to be uncomfortable to the point where you snap at others for caring about you. The goal of opening up is to make it easier for them to understand where you're coming from and help others know how to best be there for you. Most people will respect this approach. Others may press you; however, stand firm. Say the magic phrase: "I'm not willing to talk about that yet. Can we change the topic?" And if they are not willing to accept this, you can end the conversation by telling them thanks for their time and exit stage left.

We, as a society, need to normalize the grieving process. Support others by respecting what they are going through and allowing them the grace and freedom to grieve in the best way for them. We need people to feel and face their feelings in their own time.

Wearing these masks and pretending we are okay when we aren't is exhausting. We all do it and sometimes even juggle wearing multiple masks depending on where we are and who we are with. It's building up emotional toxins that seep into other areas of our lives. And we wonder why the world is chaotic. We wonder why suicide is at an all-time high. We wonder why cancer and disease are everywhere. We wonder why people are turning to alcohol, prescription, and over-the-counter drugs and numbing out any way they can. We wonder why people with anxiety, depression, and mental health are struggling. There are many reasons, and all of these are complex issues. But I feel that, as a whole, we aren't processing our pain.

When you're in the thick of your grief, allow yourself to feel your emotions. Cry if you need to cry; scream to let off some steam. Once you've acknowledged your emotions, you can start to work through them.

To do this, we need to permit ourselves to grieve authentically. This process doesn't happen overnight because we must still take care of life. You know, all those adult responsibilities. It's natural to disconnect and close ourselves off. Maybe those we typically talk to are the ones we are pushing away because they don't understand. During this process, you want to be kind and gentle to yourself.

Avoid comparing yourself to others during this time (or any time, for that matter). It's all easier said than done. *They don't know my story. They don't understand my heartache and pain. They don't have any clue what I'm going through.* You're right. They will never know precisely what you're going through because everyone's circumstances and lives differ. And they won't know how you're feeling until you let them in, either. Maybe they've never experienced that level of pain before. But when did pain become a competition?

After a loss, it can be challenging to open our hearts up to others. We want to protect ourselves from further heartache and take refuge in isolation. Yet this isn't the way God intended us to live our lives. Instead, he wants us to let others into our hearts to form meaningful connections. After all, we're here to support and love each other through this roller coaster of a journey called life. What if we get to a point where we welcome those who want to join us on that journey?

Grief impacts us in many ways; it's essential to our overall well-being to honor going through the process. Loss happens to everyone, and it's one of those experiences we wish we could opt out of, like spam in our email inbox. But I had to get to a point where I accepted that life would bring more challenges because that's how it is here on Earth.

Caregiving for my grandparents taught me a deeper level of empathy. It was one of the most challenging things I've been through, but helping them was a gift. You cannot get that time back once they leave this Earth, so to be there for them (like they were for me) was a blessing.

You may have come to a crossroads in your journey. It may be time for a reset if you are struggling. You may have isolated yourself and pushed everyone away. That's okay. Let's look at how you can transition your experience and shift your perspective. Once you do that, it will allow for greater healing to take place.

Here are a few questions to get us started:

First, who is our source?
Second, do we have a responsibility to grieve?
Third, how do we shift our perspective?
Fourth, how can we reframe our experiences?
Fifth, is there really hope when we're feeling lost?

Let's look at each of these questions.

No one can grieve for you. It's personal and private. And the masks we wear out in the world come off as soon as we step into our homes. Or maybe they come off as soon as we shower or crawl into bed. You can't hide from grief forever, as much as you may try. It will catch up to you. Ignoring it or shoving it to the side won't work either. Your distraction of choice only works for so long. I coped for years with all sorts of healthy and unhealthy methods, but I couldn't keep it up. My health and relationships took a hit. It's been a long process that required me to do the inner work needed to live a life built on a solid foundation. One way I did this was to look honestly at what sources I relied on to get through each day.

Who is your source when you need more strength? Where do you turn to when stuff hits the fan?

If your source is you, eventually, you'll run out of steam. If your source is another person in your life, you'll live in constant disappointment. If your source is the world wide web, you may find some help, but you must still decipher the misinformation and mixed messages.

When you feel lost, the way to keep your spiritual walk alive is to keep the conversation going no matter what. Closing yourself off doesn't reap any positive benefits now or later. I learned this the hard way, trial by fire. And this route can delay healing and brings no peace whatsoever. So, I encourage you to stay open. Meditate, talk, pray, or write out your thoughts and feelings.

I know that if I keep my connection to God, I can handle whatever comes my way. It will be hard. It won't be pretty. It will be messy. When I know that God is my constant, I feel safe. The realities of this world are that it is ever-changing, misleading, and temporary. But God isn't. We're the ones that pull away and change, yet God lovingly waits for us.

Sometimes we must change our view of God. From the hellfire and brimstone and God judging us all the time for what we do or don't do in our lives to one of a spiritual father that loves us, even when we aren't in the mood to reciprocate.

With each day, we have a choice. You don't have control over what happens to you. You didn't choose for your loved one to die, but it happened. And you do have a say in how you respond. I know that sounds like a glorified and overused cliché (and you are correct), but:

- You can choose to grieve or not.
- You can choose to shut people out or open your heart.
- You can choose to surrender to God or be mad at anything related to faith.
- You can see only the bad things in life instead of the blessings.
- You can choose to stay stuck or be willing to see things from different perspectives to get to a place of peace.

Sometimes it feels like the hits keep on coming. Perhaps you even feel like your life is spinning out of control. You may feel like your world is caving in right now, and you can barely breathe. Handling all the responsibilities on your plate has left you feeling emotionally and physically depleted. That's only natural.

But we have options. You can close yourself off and find a way to live with hope and possibility. To do this while you are hurting and processing your loss is astoundingly brave. It gives you warrior-level status. The easy thing to do is to drown your sorrows in anything that gets you through or enables you to forget. It tests your resolve and strength in ways you never wanted to experience. If you aren't there yet, that's cool. You will get there!

You get to play detective and find the tools that will work for you. You may have learned a few mindset shifts (like those in this book). But I wouldn't be a good coach if I said that staying emotionally stuck is okay year after year.

One of the purposes of this book is to transition your thoughts and shift your mindset so that you start viewing the losses that life has handed you differently. Does it make it easy? Nope. Will there be days you want to hide under the covers? Yep. I still have some of those myself. But the point is that you *start* to see and move your life in the direction of hope and possibility. It's not a switch—one day, you grieve, and the next day, week, or year, you will be fine. Of course, it can take time and doesn't happen instantaneously, but it can and will if you are open to it.

So what's the key to having an open heart? It's living from a state of willingness and surrendering your deepest fears and hurt to God.

Know that this is a day-by-day exercise (perhaps even a moment-by-moment exercise). When you cut off your emotions and choose not to feel them, you are cutting the lines of communication with yourself and God. God can handle any feelings you might have in your life. So don't give up on your faith or yourself—power through the moments when you feel you won't make it. You're not alone even when you feel alone.

Ask yourself this question. Why are you unwilling to consider a new viewpoint—stuck in your ways? You don't want to change? Are you afraid? Afraid of what? To let go? Afraid of change? Afraid to forget? Fearful because the memories are fading? Do you feel like you can no longer hear their voice? You haven't, and you won't. It's all there inside of you.

But you get stuck when fear runs a tape of doubt in your mind.

As you know, I'm all for facing our feelings, but it's important to realize something. Feelings aren't always facts. They are valid for you, but sometimes you don't always see things clearly in your pain. We take that information and write a story about it, so it becomes our version of truth. That doesn't make what you are going through right or wrong. Because what you are experiencing is entirely valid. But look at it this way.

Have you ever craved food that you couldn't eat because of allergies? If you have a severe nut allergy, you must stay away from them. But what if a craving hits and you feel like eating those little tasty, salty treats? After all, they are healthy and provide nutritional benefits, right? But in your situation, even though you *feel* like eating nuts and maybe even crave them, they are dangerous. You have an allergy, and if you partake, you could suffer severe consequences to your body. So even in this extreme example, sometimes, feelings aren't always aligned with facts, and our minds find facts to justify and support our opinions about any topic.

Therefore, relying solely on our feelings isn't always the best option. It's essential to be a willing vessel and remain open to what we can learn from every experience. It's true even for those situations that leave us feeling broken and hurting, which leaves a massive hole in our hearts. It's possible to learn and love while grieving at the same time.

Sometimes, to find wisdom after chaos, we need to humble ourselves. First, it's accepting that we don't have control and we don't know everything. It means understanding that we don't see the bigger universal picture and we can't do everything in our strength by ourselves.

Is that comforting? Not really. But it's the truth. If this isn't connecting with you today, that's okay. Your feelings aren't wrong, and what I'm saying isn't either. That's why grief and life is a personal journey.

You aren't alone either, my friend. People are wearing invisible masks everywhere we go. Even when talking with Bible believers or people with a strong faith and spiritual life, the fake happiness seems to ooze out. It's as if we must appear happy, or else we don't have enough faith. The catch is that fakeness drives people away.

How can we expect to be there for others when we push them away with our pretentious perfectionism? Pretending you are all fine and dandy at church, you go home, take off those Sunday best clothes, crumple on the couch, or get mouthy and snappy. You can't be polished, pretend your life is amazing, and then live the other six days in crisis. We've all done it, but we can do better—me included! It's time to raise the standards with compassion, empathy, and kindness. Being honest with people goes a long way, and it starts with being able to admit where we've fallen short and the willingness to do better.

But if we remove our masks, what good will come of it? Can there be beauty from the ashes when one is grieving?

As I went through the caregiving process, I wasn't thinking how glad I was for the experience. That perspective took some time and distance. I knew that I was grateful to be able to help, but seeing all the blessings during the trial wasn't happening in real time.

But with perspective, it taught me how to reprioritize what's truly important and live a life where it's not all about me. Instead, it's about being there and showing up for the ones you love and people who cross your path by encouraging each other, especially during difficult times. It's what helped me find meaning in the madness.

Does that mean you will always feel happy? Nope.

Does that mean you will not get triggered by grief? No.

Does that mean that grief's sting will leave you be? Probably not.

The loss of something or someone in your life can be devastating. It can leave your heart shattered and torn to pieces. But pretending you are fine when you aren't isn't the answer.

So, what can we do? Think about honoring their memory throughout the process:

- It's about thanking God for the gift of that person in your life.
- It's about finding tools that work with where you are today in your grief journey.
- It's about finding a sense of gratitude for what you are learning and who you are becoming because of the precious moments you shared with your loved one.

That's the start of reframing your mindset. So, then, all it takes is simply getting to the place where you say, "I am willing to be open to what this experience can teach me, even though I've never experienced such heartbreak and don't know how to go on."

If you can get to that place, that's a huge win! Then, we can be open and willing to see things from new points of view, and we can dive deeper by asking ourselves some questions that will help us gain further insights from our experiences. It's all a process, but this will allow us to uncover hidden meanings we can apply to our lives, connect with God, and view the world around us.

- How did this person add to my life?
- What did they teach me while they were alive?
- How can I honor their memory?
- What am I afraid of now that they are gone?
- How has God been there for me in the past?
- Has God helped me through dark times before?
- How do I connect and draw closer to my higher power?

When you're ready, write and answer these questions in your journal. If you find yourself lost or overwhelmed, write one question daily. Allow your answer to flow naturally. Try not to rush the process. You may find that nothing is coming to you. If that's the case, write down the question and walk away. Sometimes the answers will come, and pearls of wisdom will spring to mind as you go throughout the day. When that happens, go back to your journal and write them down.

It's about discovering that activity that will allow you to get out what you're holding inside in a healthy way. If something doesn't work, try something else. Sometimes we need to put in a little effort to find the tools that will work for us. Everyone is different, and a cookie-cutter approach rarely works, so explore your go-to.

Many years ago, a book was recommended to me called *One Thousand Gifts* by Ann Voskamp. It's the author's story about finding blessings in everyday life. It wasn't a thrilling page-turner, but it was insightful and made me think about my life—which was probably the point.

At the end of the book, the author encourages you to write down one thousand gifts from your life. Of course, we often write down the "big" and most obvious things in our lives. But this exercise stretches you to start thinking about the everyday, mundane things that we may skip over or often go unnoticed. So, I took on the challenge and dedicated a journal to writing one thousand gifts.

The whole process reminded me that when we are going through our darkest times that we often forget the blessings God has given to us. Looking back is a means of reflecting on what we learned, but seeing the good can remind us that God was with us. He carried us through these other storms, and God can, and will, do the same now.

Chances are you've gone through some painful situations—a breakup, a family member's death, divorce, job loss, a friendship that no longer exists, etc. What happened? Did you get through it? Are you still standing? Do you think about those experiences differently since they happened one, five, fifteen, or twenty years ago?

Writing these down and reviewing this list when you're questioning, doubting, and hurting can be a reminder of what you've already gone through in the past. If God brought you through those experiences, won't God do the same now? Combining your blessings and difficulties in the same journal is an excellent reminder of everything you've gone through.

Allowing yourself to fully feel is freedom. But it's a process and doesn't happen overnight. There is no microwave-quick solution to grief. But how you choose to think about grief *will* make a difference.

To have an open heart doesn't mean that you have to share your business with everyone you meet. It means opening your heart to God first, then others when you're ready. If you don't talk to the other person in a relationship, it will fall to pieces and become nonexistent. God can handle raw honesty (check out the book of Psalms). God can handle our humanness. So bring it all on, and keep the lines of communication open.

After a loss or death, it's easy to shut down. You walk around like a member of the living dead. You're going through the motions, but you're not feeling anything. We do the things we need to do daily, but we're numb. If our hurting hearts let up, we know a meltdown is inevitable. It's easier to harden our hearts rather than hope. Do you feel that your hope is gone? Perhaps your head hangs down in discouragement more often than you look up. After all, the weight of the burdens you are carrying is heavy.

After my grandfather died, there was a lot to do. Although I couldn't attend the funeral in person, I managed to get back to Florida a few days afterward, once I knew I didn't have COVID. Caregiving is overwhelming, but everything after that is equally challenging. You are making various arrangements, organizing, and sifting through the chaos.

Meanwhile, your family is putting in their requests for what they want. You have well-wishers bringing over meals. You have a lot of legal and financial mumbo-jumbo to figure out. You are dealing with the emotions of it all; sometimes, it becomes too much.

One day, as I was organizing and filling the boxes with everyone's requested items from my grandparents' house, I reached up to pull down this poem that was etched on a piece of wood. It had been on the wall for years and years. I never really stopped to read it. But that day, I did, and it brought tears to my eyes. It reassured me that a power greater than this universe is with me no matter what I'm going through right now.

Margaret Fishback Power is the author of this classic and timeless poem, "Footprints in the Sand." Have you ever read the entire thing? Here it is:

One night, I dreamed a dream. I was walking along the beach with my Lord. Across the dark sky flashed scenes from my life.

For each scene, I noticed two sets of footprints in the sand, one belonging to me and one to my Lord.

When the last scene of my life shot before me, I looked back at the footprints in the sand. There was only one set of footprints. I realized that this was at the lowest and saddest times of my life. This always bothered me, and I questioned the Lord about my dilemma.

"Lord, You told me when I decided to follow You, You would walk and talk with me all the way. But I'm aware that during the most troublesome times of my life, there is only one set of footprints. I just don't understand why, when I need You most, You leave me."

He whispered, "My precious child, I love you and will never leave you, never, ever, during your trials and testings. When you saw only one set of footprints, it was then that I carried you."

Truth time: sometimes I forget God is there with me through those dark and difficult seasons. I deal with it or figure it out on my own. I don't want to burden anyone else with it, so I put on that mask and say that everything is good, even when it's not. When I feel that anxiousness creep in, it's because I am not making time for those moments where I reconnect with the One who created the universe. That's why it's crucial to get still, calm our minds, and reconnect spiritually.

Living with an open heart or shutting out the world is a daily choice. Some days you'll need time and space to be alone; however, you can remain open to what God is showing you through the process. Remembering that God carries us through the darkest times of our lives, whether we realize it or not, can bring us some comfort and hope.

My loving nudge to you now is this: everyone is different. There is no right or wrong way to be. It can be difficult not to compare your situation to others, but it's important to remember that everyone has a unique path. No matter how it seems from the outside, everyone is dealing with their heartache and pain.

CHAPTER 12

Memories

We started out saying that this was a journey. It's much more than that; it's an adventure. With a journey, you have a destination in mind. You may even have a map showing how to get from Point A to Point B. But with an adventure, there is a risk. There is uncertainty. You don't have a map. You take the next best step. Life is an adventure because we have no idea what is in store for us. That's both exciting and scary.

Human beings love to be in control. But we need to realize that we have very little power and must seek the One who holds the universe together. God doesn't cause bad things to happen. Because we live in a fallen, imperfect world, some things happen to us and to the people we love that make absolutely no sense. There is no rhyme or reason to any of it.

When I'm wondering where God is amid the chaos, I go outside and look up at the sky. In nature, I always feel a presence that is bigger than myself. It brings me back to life again. A spiritual knowing that a powerful force created this universe and that I'm part of the bigger picture, just like those who came before me and will arrive on this Earth long after me.

Because of what you have been through and what you are still going through, chances are you are not the same person as before. You have evolved, whether you wanted to or not. Why? Because your loved one has moved on from this life and is no longer here. That is a considerable change. And because of that loss, your life has been forever changed. There is no going back. You're forced to adapt to a new reality you didn't want to face. But you do have a choice on how you process and view grief. The question becomes: will you keep wearing those masks, or will you make a conscious decision to work through the painful emotions and allow the process to unfold?

Let's recap a few things that we've learned along our literary journey.

We've reviewed society's common clichés and typical responses when a loved one dies. We have learned to show compassion for the emotions, feelings, and thoughts we may still have lingering about our loved ones. We have become hyperaware that our grief has a multi-layered impact on our lives.

We realize that we don't have control, and our go-to ways of coping could have long-term effects on ourselves and others. We know that an attitude of surrender is needed to allow for greater inner healing. We have learned to release the negative and unresolved conversations that repeatedly replay in our minds.

We now see the importance of communicating with those around us that can keep our hearts open, allowing us to grieve more authentically and freely. We understand that there will be times when we feel like we are going backward, especially around key milestones or memories that come each calendar year.

We covered how to reframe our grief, so we can unveil moments of gratitude by asking questions like: What did they teach me? What memory will be forever imprinted on my heart? What lesson did their love show me about the world? You need to focus on that individual's positive impact on your life. This exercise helps you find moments in your grieving journey to focus on the good.

We reviewed how to live from a place of willingness so our hearts do not become bitter and hardened. Of course, it's never an easy thing to do when we feel immense heartache, pain, and sadness. But, over time, this can allow us to embrace our pain and rediscover life from new perspectives, which is one essential key to healing.

And we know that sometimes the things we go through in this life have a greater purpose beyond our understanding. So grief, and life, is there to teach and guide us.

All of these things combined give us a greater appreciation for our fellow human beings. No one is immune, because we all experience hardship, trials, and grief. This realization will help us become more compassionate, empathetic, and kinder to those who come across our paths, whether they are in our lives for a fleeting moment, a month, a year, or a lifetime.

All of this is challenging. Words like "moving forward," "get on with life," "healing from grief," and "rediscovering joy" are difficult phrases to swallow when your heart is hurting. But wearing a mask and pretending to be okay isn't the answer. Suppressing our emotions and numbing our feelings with our coping mechanism of choice won't work long term, either.

This book is not telling you how to grieve. Instead, the purpose is to show you that what you are going through is okay and that we don't always have to pretend. It's to let you know that it's normal to feel all of the emotions you are experiencing, even ones like anger. You just want to make sure that you avoid stalling out and staying stuck in anger, sadness, and sorrow. The key is being in tune and aware of what you are going through instead of ignoring it.

That awareness can help you recognize the emotional patterns that you are doing every day that may no longer be serving you. Instead, they are making you feel imprisoned with no way out. Although this road will have ups and downs, you can make it.

You may be feeling resistance when reading some of this material; that's cool. Some of it may need extra time to sink in. Although I've found these to be spot on, some things may not be applicable, and for others, you may need more time to digest them. We're all in different places. As you go through your journey, you may find other truths that make better sense or work better for you.

In life, we all have choices. You have a choice to make too. You can allow the contents of this book to sink in and take the time to answer the questions laced throughout this book, so that you can excavate and chip away at the walls you built on the inside of you. Or you can shut the book, say, "This is stupid," throw it in the giveaway pile, and continue repeating the same behaviors and allowing the same emotional war to keep raging within you.

If you've been battling with grief for a while and are still feeling trapped, the steps that we reviewed can help you begin to transition your thoughts on grief into something more productive. Some of this may not be a fit depending on where you are at in life. So, take what you need for where you are now and leave the rest. But when you step back, I hope that you find that grief and this life are not enemies. Instead, it is a guide and a teacher—albeit a really mean one, at times.

Speaking of teachers, one of the questions we love to ask God (and teachers) is, "Why?" But if you want an answer for "why" something happened or you're waiting for an easy microwave-solution to work through the pain that you are experiencing, you will be disappointed. Unfortunately, there is no easy fix to grief, life, or loss. You may never understand why something happened or why it makes no sense. Grief, and everything that comes along with it, is complex. Accepting these hard truths may seem impossible, but once you do, you can find your footing again and, in time, discover a renewed sense of hope, peace, and purpose.

You may not be there today; however, if you open your heart and mind to even the slightest possibility, you will get there. You just might need a little bit of help. Doing things on your own is a hard habit to break. Does anyone else have the lone wolf gene? Both my hands are raised. It's where you try to handle things on your own. You push, pull, dig in your heels, and power through the mud and the muck until you get to the other side. But you didn't realize that you could've taken another route.

It took me years to get to a point where I admitted that I needed to talk to someone. But eventually, I did. It wasn't a magic wand; however, over time, I noticed that talking with someone not in my everyday life, a complete third party, helped me become generous with others, emotionally grounded, and more productive.

There is more than one way to grieve or cope with loss. Whether we want it to be or not, grief is both a teacher and guide. But unlike school, there are no exams. There is no pass or fail. Sometimes it feels like we are moving five steps forward, only to be knocked ten steps back. This constant up-and-down battle is exhausting and makes you feel defeated. But in these moments of testing, don't give up on yourself or others. You're gonna make it. You're gonna be okay.

When I look at the root cause regarding the things that I've run away from over the years, it comes down to stuffing down and overriding my emotions to get on with my life. But we're not robots. We have real, challenging things that we each face. And grieving life's losses along the way is essential so we can live from a place of authenticity.

Grief has no set timetable. There is no right way or wrong way to grieve. It's a complex, personal, and private journey that no one can walk for us. Yet, in some ways, we will always be grieving the losses of life. That's why we need tools to address these aspects of life. Some of those tools we've learned so far:

- Importance of journaling.
- Writing letters to resolve lingering emotions or trauma.
- Talking with a few trusted friends.
- Finding professional support.

In addition, I want to mention the importance of self-care. It's one of those popular phrases you hear, but having go-to rituals can prevent emotional burnout. Sometimes it feels impossible to add in things that seem like extra indulgences. We think that we have no energy, time, or money. But when we are grieving, it's vital to do something special for yourself that you can work into your daily, weekly, or monthly routines.

Think of things that relax you and, preferably, are screen-free. Here are some examples: gardening, massage, meditation, facials, yoga, bubble bath, baking, hiking, picnic at the park, special coffee/tea, pedicures, manicure, or anything that makes you feel special and cared for.

Pick at least one thing you can do regularly—anything to show yourself a little love when you are having a tough day. Loving ourselves is an important step that often gets overlooked. Once we do, our hearts are repositioned, and we're ready to be there for others. Though the road has ups and downs, God will be there every step of the way, if we let Him. God will carry the heaviness of our grief so we can embrace life with more kindness, generosity, and vulnerability.

It's time to view ourselves through that empathetic lens. I hesitated to bring this next step up. You may not be ready for it. But I think that it would be a disservice if I didn't share.

There will come a point in time when you may reach a plateau in your grief. You have worked through your emotions, your heart is open, and you are willing to see your sorrow from different points of view, but you feel like your progress is stalling even though you've done a lot of inner work.

So, what's next? At this stage, consider sharing your story and passing on the wisdom that you've gained through your experiences.

Grief stays with you and will not end until we pass from this life to the next. But grief can evolve, soften, and teach us over time. And what would happen if we could use our grief for good somehow?

If death or loss happened recently, this probably is not your default mindset. Instead, your mood is more like: *I'm hurting; I miss them; I want them back; this isn't fair; I'm mad at (fill in the blank); I don't think I can go on; I don't want my life to be without this person;* and a plethora of other horrible and difficult thoughts.

As time goes on, these feelings may remain; however, they usually soften as one navigates life. Nevertheless, you feel surrounded by a heaviness that you cannot explain. So, if that's you, the invitation is to create a mindset of wonder.

There are different ways wonder can come into play. Seeing things come to life through the eyes of a child can brighten the gloomiest of rooms. For instance, observe how they act when they see a Christmas tree full of lights and sparkle, emit high-pitched squeals at an amusement park, or get excited about ice cream. Unfortunately, most adults lose this childlike wonder as the realities of life set in. Wonder can also come in the form of intrigue and speculation, which we will focus on. The idea is to use an "I wonder if..." phrase at the beginning of your thoughts. It trains your brain to think in the form of questions, possibilities, and solutions.

- *I wonder if my story can help others.*
- *I wonder what I learned so far.*
- *I wonder if this grief is showing me something about my purpose here on Earth.*
- *I wonder if this grief is showing me how to improve my relationships.*

- *I wonder how I can make more of a difference.*
- *I wonder if I could be more empathetic and treat others with compassion and kindness.*

It's about taking a step forward. One that is often very scary and uncomfortable. You've gone through a lot, and you've learned a lot of things. Perhaps you want to help someone else but are afraid you are not far enough along in your grief to really be an encouragement because you feel like you aren't "there" yet.

Here's the thing: you'll never really be ready. You can always find a reason not to take the extra step. On my journey, I hit a plateau. I could handle the emotions of life, relationships, and all the other difficult things. But I still felt like I needed to do something else. I just didn't know what. It wasn't until I opened up to other people about what I was going through that I felt a release. Some of the lingering internal pressure was finally going away. It was incredibly challenging, and I got a bit emotional. You may want to consider sharing your story if you find yourself hitting a wall with your grief. Especially if you get the sense that there is another level of healing, but you don't know what to do or how to get there.

The first step is being open and considering the idea. It takes time to reach a point where we have the humility and emotional capacity to share our hearts. If you're even remotely thinking about doing this, that's commendable. If you aren't there yet, please know that's okay.

Sharing isn't about dispensing advice or being a know-it-all. It's simply encouraging others, loving those around you, and showing up for the people in your life. We often make the act of service this big, monumental gesture—like feeding an entire country. The truth is, most of us can make a bigger difference in our backyard, local communities.

It starts with one person. Planting a seed of hope in others will bring you to another level of healing. It will teach you something new and help widen your perspective more than you can imagine. That doesn't mean you have to start a business, become a coach, write a book, or do something that isn't your thing. You can stay true to who you are, using your gifts and talents for those in your corner of the world. What you love and what you're good at is always important.

For example, if you love to cook, why don't you surprise a struggling neighbor with a home-cooked meal or a batch of your favorite sweet treats? You may love baking, throwing a party, painting, or teaching. Those things can all benefit others—and you can benefit from sharing that light with them. What if you could brighten someone's day with something as simple as a smile and a handwritten card? It's all about finding a way to help and support those around you that feels natural, not forced.

In today's world, it's easy to find something to argue about or something nasty to say about someone on social media. But what if we picked a different approach? What if we realized that no matter our background, race, beliefs, education, or lifestyle, everyone is going through something difficult? What if we stopped making assumptions about other people's lives? What if we let people off the hook? What if you let yourself off the hook? What if we chose to see God's goodness in life, even when having a crappy day, week, month, or year?

We all have a path to walk, and that path is filled with challenges, obstacles, and minefields. Everyone is walking through their own minefield. It's why those small gestures have the biggest impact. Something as simple as an encouraging word can lift the spirits of someone struggling with depression and loneliness. And as counterintuitive as it sounds, it helps you heal in ways that you never knew you needed!

As your journey continues, remember:

- Grief is a guide.
- Grief allows us to see the world through a different and even spiritual lens.
- Grief can ground us in gratitude for our past, present, and future.
- Grief can lead us to support others *when we're ready* and in ways that honor our natural gifts and talents.

Grief differs across the globe, and learning about other cultures is fascinating. For example, my father shared a Jewish phrase that people often say when a loved one passes from this life to the next.

"May their memory be a blessing."

Isn't that beautiful? No relationship is perfect. It's not always sunshine and roses, but there is an opportunity to see even the most dysfunctional relationships as a chance to grow in our human experience. Even if we learn all the things *not* to do, that is still a gift available for us. And that can give way to gratitude in time.

That person impacted your life. To honor them, focus on the good, carry them with you, and then pass on what you've learned from them to others. Let's love ourselves and each other, always remembering the good.

Grief is a burden that you don't have to carry on your own. Remember:

- God is always there, even if you can't feel or see Him.
- Seek extra support through a coach, counselor, or licensed professional if you continue to struggle, and remember you are never alone.
- Take the time to grieve authentically, fully, and freely. It's vital for your emotional, mental, physical, and spiritual well-being.

And may the memory of your loved one forever be a blessing.

CHAPTER 13

Beyond Death

What if you are grieving the loss of something other than the death of a loved one? You may wonder if these tools in this book apply. They are just as relevant.

My car accident in 2006 was the spark that lit the flame leading me down the path of health and wellness. It's been a process of self-discovery and exploration. I count myself blessed because my accident could have been much worse, but that doesn't mean it was easy. When you find yourself with chronic pain that you can't escape, it wears you down. You get desperate and are willing to try almost anything so you aren't in pain, even if only for a little while.

I tested and tried various forms of Eastern and Western medicine. I followed the orders from my US-based doctors exactly to the letter. But it wasn't helping. Their answer was throwing pain pills at me. I knew something was wrong, but they wouldn't listen. They kept saying it was whiplash.

Six months after my car accident I was driving to Houston to visit one of my best friends. I spent the entire three-hour drive crying from pain. Thankfully, I was able to get in to see a doctor in Houston. They discovered the disc herniation that my other doctors in Austin missed. Finally, I had an answer. When I went back home, I started physical therapy and was told if I did all of these exercises that I would no longer be in pain. So naively taking the word of my doctors, I signed my insurance settlement. That was in 2006, and I still have pain today.

Over the years I learned to adapt; however, some days are easier than others. The things we go through may be difficult to digest; however, they can lead us down unexpected roads.

Because I couldn't get the relief from my doctors after years of doing it their way, I decided enough was enough. I rolled up my sleeves and tried to figure out my pain issues myself.

Drinking wine and whisky helped temporarily, but had unwanted side effects. The pills they gave me were the only thing that helped me sleep that led to a slight addiction. Dating men as a distraction worked, but because of my emotional unavailability, I attracted the same.

So after a while, I switched gears. I researched and read books, which ultimately led me to studying with Cynthia Garcia at the Institute of Transformational Nutrition. I received a health coaching certification, and with my ambitious self, I didn't stop there. I have certifications in corporate wellness, aromatherapy, holistic health, and grief coaching.

Here are a few eye-opening lessons I learned going through my chronic pain journey:

1) It's a long road filled with trial and error. Basically, you end up being your own guinea pig or lab rat.

You test the foods you eat, beverages you drink, and supplements to see what might take the edge off the constant, never-ending pain. I stopped and started so many things because I wasn't seeing the results. In addition, I tried chiropractic care, acupuncture, gua sha (or scraping), Ayurveda, traditional Chinese medicine, many types of massage, infrared heating pads, and others. It can get discouraging, but don't give up.

2) It's more than just being physical. It took me a while to figure this one out. But when I discovered that there was an emotional, mental, and spiritual component to healing, that's when I started to notice a difference. It's all connected, and that's why we need an inside-outside approach.

3) You have to become your own healthcare advocate. The healthcare system is chaotic, corrupt, and tricky. You may hear disheartening comments from family, friends, and even physicians. "There is nothing wrong with you." "You look fine." "Maybe it's in your head." A doctor told me that once. While that was infuriating, I knew I had to figure it out myself because the doctors didn't want to deal with it. No one cares as much as you do about the pain you're living in. You need to take the bull by the horns. If you have questions, be bold and ask your doctor. If you aren't sure if alternative medicine is covered by your insurance, get on the phone and check. If you want to learn more about a new healing technique, find someone who has done it and scour the reviews. The options are out there, and endless.

4) There's more than one singular solution. Usually, it's a combination of techniques that work together to provide relief. I haven't ever been pain-free since my car accident; however, I have figured out how to reduce it. Next, I had to adjust my expectations and adapt to my circumstances. Resisting the pain and refusing to accept additional diagnoses like fibromyalgia (which was triggered by my car accident and subsequent bad habits) made things worse. You have to become aware and accept where you are in life today. And most importantly, don't give up.

All of these lessons apply to grief as well. There is no one-size-fits-all answer. The depth of pain impacts us on many levels. You have to be your own advocate. And there will never be one thing that helps you grieve. It will take many things working in tandem over time.

(Chronic disease and pain, or invisible illnesses, are topics I'm passionate about. That'll be another book or two in the future, so connect with me on <u>alisonbrehme.com</u> to stay updated.)

Acknowledgments

To thank all the people who have supported me on this journey could fill a book. I'm grateful for the dark and difficult times in my life because, without those experiences, this book would not have come to light.

To my family, friends, and co-workers who have passed from this life to the next, thank you for touching my life. You each left an imprint on my life. Although I can't rewind time to tell you how much you meant to me, I can carry you in my heart and memories.

Thank you to my parents, who always supported me, even when my decisions didn't make sense.

Thank you to my coaches, family, and friends who cheered me on from the sidelines. I'm blessed and grateful for each of you.

Author Bio

Alison Brehme is a certified Grief and Joy Restoration Coach, aromatherapist, holistic health, nutrition, and corporate wellness coach, but she started her corporate career in advertising and marketing with Fortune 500 technology companies. She was a true workaholic until a series of deaths in the family shook her worldview. Through a tumultuous season of grief (and trying to ignore her grief), she finally found the benefits of vulnerability and truly feeling her emotions. God shifted her focus from the corporate world to family, and there was no going back. Today, she helps others navigate their emotions and access their own vulnerability rather than try to bypass grief with work or other distractions. That's why she turned her focus to the written word to try to help as many people as possible. Her written work can be found in Corporate Wellness Magazine and on Well.org. This is her first book on this topic. When she is not teaching or learning about emotional and holistic health, she can be found traveling, doing yoga, or enjoying a beautiful sunset. You can find out more about her here: www.alisonbrehme.com

URGENT PLEA!

Thank You For Reading My Book!

I really appreciate all of your feedback and
I love hearing what you have to say.

I need your input to make the next version of
this book and my future books better.

Please take two minutes now to leave a helpful review on
Amazon letting me know what you thought of the book.

Thanks so much!
- Alison Brehme